THE PELICAN SHAKESPEARE
GENERAL EDITORS

STEPHEN ORGEL
A. R. BRAUNMULLER

The Tragedy of Julius Caesar

The Irish actor Thomas Sheridan (father of the playwright Richard Brinsley Sheridan) in his most famous role as Brutus, first performed at Covent Garden in 1744. His manner was cool, formal, and intellectual, admirably suited to Brutus, though he was criticized for lacking Garrick's naturalness. From Bell's Shakespeare (1773–76).

William Shakespeare

The Tragedy of
Julius Caesar

EDITED BY WILLIAM MONTGOMERY
WITH AN INTRODUCTION BY DOUGLAS TREVOR

PENGUIN BOOKS

PENGUIN BOOKS

Published by the Penguin Group

Penguin Group (USA) Inc., 375 Hudson Street, New York, New York 10014, U.S.A.

Penguin Books Ltd, 80 Strand, London WC2R 0RL, England

Penguin Books Australia Ltd, 250 Camberwell Road, Camberwell, Victoria 3124, Australia

Penguin Books Canada Ltd, 10 Alcorn Avenue, Toronto, Ontario, Canada M4V 3B2

Penguin Books India (P) Ltd, 11 Community Centre, Panchsheel Park, New Delhi – 110 017, India

Penguin Books (N.Z.) Ltd, Cnr Rosedale and Airborne Roads, Albany, Auckland, New Zealand

Penguin Books (South Africa) (Pty) Ltd, 24 Sturdee Avenue,
Rosebank, Johannesburg 2196, South Africa

Penguin Books Ltd, Registered Offices: 80 Strand, London WC2R 0RL, England

Julius Caesar edited by S. F. Johnson published in the
United States of America in Penguin Books 1960
Revised edition published 1971
This new edition edited by William Montgomery with an
introduction by Douglas Trevor published 2000

20 19 18 17 16 15 14 13 12 11

Copyright © Penguin Books Inc., 1960, 1971
Copyright © Penguin Putnam Inc., 2000
All rights reserved

ISBN 0-14-07.1468-5
[CIP data available]

Printed in the United States of America
Set in Adobe Garamond
Designed by Virginia Norey

Contents

Publisher's Note

IT IS ALMOST half a century since the first volumes of the Pelican Shakespeare appeared under the general editorship of Alfred Harbage. The fact that a new edition, rather than simply a revision, has been undertaken reflects the profound changes textual and critical studies of Shakespeare have undergone in the past twenty years. For the new Pelican series, the texts of the plays and poems have been thoroughly revised in accordance with recent scholarship, and in some cases have been entirely reedited. New introductions and notes have been provided in all the volumes. But the new Shakespeare is also designed as a successor to the original series; the previous editions have been taken into account, and the advice of the previous editors has been solicited where it was feasible to do so.

Certain textual features of the new Pelican Shakespeare should be particularly noted. All lines are numbered that contain a word, phrase, or allusion explained in the glossarial notes. In addition, for convenience, every tenth line is also numbered, in italics when no annotation is indicated. The intrusive and often inaccurate place headings inserted by early editors are omitted (as is becoming standard practice), but for the convenience of those who miss them, an indication of locale now appears as the first item in the annotation of each scene.

In the interest of both elegance and utility, each speech prefix is set in a separate line when the speaker's lines are in verse, except when those words form the second half of a verse line. Thus the verse form of the speech is kept visually intact. What is printed as verse and what is printed as prose has, in general, the authority of the original texts. Departures from the original texts in this regard have only the authority of editorial tradition and the judgment of the Pelican editors; and, in a few instances, are admittedly arbitrary.

The Theatrical World

ECONOMIC REALITIES determined the theatrical world in which Shakespeare's plays were written, performed, and received. For centuries in England, the primary theatrical tradition was nonprofessional. Craft guilds (or "mysteries") provided religious drama – mystery plays – as part of the celebration of religious and civic festivals, and schools and universities staged classical and neoclassical drama in both Latin and English as part of their curricula. In these forms, drama was established and socially acceptable. Professional theater, in contrast, existed on the margins of society. The acting companies were itinerant; playhouses could be any available space – the great halls of the aristocracy, town squares, civic halls, inn yards, fair booths, or open fields – and income was sporadic, dependent on the passing of the hat or on the bounty of local patrons. The actors, moreover, were considered little better than vagabonds, constantly in danger of arrest or expulsion.

In the late 1560s and 1570s, however, English professional theater began to gain respectability. Wealthy aristocrats fond of drama – the Lord Admiral, for example, or the Lord Chamberlain – took acting companies under their protection so that the players technically became members of their households and were no longer subject to arrest as homeless or masterless men. Permanent theaters were first built at this time as well, allowing the companies to control and charge for entry to their performances.

Shakespeare's livelihood, and the stunning artistic explosion in which he participated, depended on pragmatic and architectural effort. Professional theater requires ways to restrict access to its offerings; if it does not, and admission fees cannot be charged, the actors do not get paid, the costumes go to a pawnbroker, and there is no such thing as a professional, ongoing theatrical tradition. The answer to that economic need arrived in the late 1560s and 1570s with the creation of the so-called public or amphitheater playhouse. Recent discoveries indicate that the precursor of the Globe playhouse in London (where Shakespeare's mature plays were presented) and the Rose theater (which presented Christopher Marlowe's plays and some of Shakespeare's earliest ones) was the Red Lion theater of 1567. Archaeological studies of the foundations of the Rose and Globe theaters have revealed that the open-air theater of the 1590s and later was probably a polygonal building with fourteen to twenty or twenty-four sides, multistoried, from 75 to 100 feet in diameter, with a raised, partly covered "thrust" stage that projected into a group of standing patrons, or "groundlings," and a covered gallery, seating up to 2,500 or more (very crowded) spectators.

These theaters might have been about half full on any given day, though the audiences were larger on holidays or when a play was advertised, as old and new were, through printed playbills posted around London. The metropolitan area's late-Tudor, early-Stuart population (circa 1590–1620) has been estimated at about 150,000 to 250,000. It has been supposed that in the mid-1590s there were about 15,000 spectators per week at the public theaters; thus, as many as 10 percent of the local population went to the theater regularly. Consequently, the theaters' repertories – the plays available for this experienced and frequent audience – had to change often: in the month between September 15 and October 15, 1595, for instance, the Lord Admiral's Men performed twenty-eight times in eighteen different plays.

Since natural light illuminated the amphitheaters' stages, performances began between noon and two o'clock and ran without a break for two or three hours. They often concluded with a jig, a fencing display, or some other nondramatic exhibition. Weather conditions determined the season for the amphitheaters: plays were performed every day (including Sundays, sometimes, to clerical dismay) except during Lent – the forty days before Easter – or periods of plague, or sometimes during the summer months when law courts were not in session and the most affluent members of the audience were not in London.

To a modern theatergoer, an amphitheater stage like that of the Rose or Globe would appear an unfamiliar mixture of plainness and elaborate decoration. Much of the structure was carved or painted, sometimes to imitate marble; elsewhere, as under the canopy projecting over the stage, to represent the stars and the zodiac. Appropriate painted canvas pictures (of Jerusalem, for example, if the play was set in that city) were apparently hung on the wall behind the acting area, and tragedies were accompanied by black hangings, presumably something like crepe festoons or bunting. Although these theaters did not employ what we would call scenery, early modern spectators saw numerous large props, such as the "bar" at which a prisoner stood during a trial, the "mossy bank" where lovers reclined, an arbor for amorous conversation, a chariot, gallows, tables, trees, beds, thrones, writing desks, and so forth. Audiences might learn a scene's location from a sign (reading "Athens," for example) carried across the stage (as in Bertolt Brecht's twentieth-century productions). Equally captivating (and equally irritating to the theater's enemies) were the rich costumes and personal props the actors used: the most valuable items in the surviving theatrical inventories are the swords, gowns, robes, crowns, and other items worn or carried by the performers.

Magic appealed to Shakespeare's audiences as much as it does to us today, and the theater exploited many deceptive and spectacular devices. A winch in the loft above the stage, called "the heavens," could lower and raise actors playing gods, goddesses, and other supernatural figures to and from the main acting area, just as one or more trapdoors permitted entrances and exits to and from the area, called "hell," beneath the stage. Actors wore elementary makeup such as wigs, false beards, and face paint, and they employed pig's bladders filled with animal blood to make wounds seem more real. They had rudimentary but effective ways of pretending to behead or hang a person. Supernumeraries (stagehands or actors not needed in a particular scene) could make thunder sounds (by shaking a metal sheet or rolling an iron ball down a chute) and show lightning (by blowing inflammable resin through tubes into a flame). Elaborate fireworks enhanced the effects of dragons flying through the air or imitated such celestial phenomena as comets, shooting stars, and multiple suns. Horses' hoofbeats, bells (located perhaps in the tower above the stage), trumpets and drums, clocks, cannon shots and gunshots, and the like were common sound effects. And the music of viols, cornets, oboes, and recorders was a regular feature of theatrical performances.

For two relatively brief spans, from the late 1570s to 1590 and from 1599 to 1614, the amphitheaters competed with the so-called private, or indoor, theaters, which originated as, or later represented themselves as, educational institutions training boys as singers for church services and court performances. These indoor theaters had two features that were distinct from the amphitheaters': their personnel and their playing spaces. The amphitheaters' adult companies included both adult men, who played the male roles, and boys, who played the female roles; the private, or indoor, theater companies, on the other hand, were entirely composed of boys aged about 8 to 16, who were, or could pretend to be, candidates for singers in a church or a royal boys' choir. (Until 1660, professional theatrical companies included no women.) The playing space would appear much more familiar to modern audiences than the long-vanished amphitheaters; the later indoor theaters were, in fact, the ancestors of the typical modern theater. They were enclosed spaces, usually rectangular, with the stage filling one end of the rectangle and the audience arrayed in seats or benches across (and sometimes lining) the building's longer axis. These spaces staged plays less frequently than the public theaters (perhaps only once a week) and held far fewer spectators than the amphitheaters: about 200 to 600, as opposed to 2,500 or more. Fewer patrons mean a smaller gross income, unless each pays more. Not surprisingly, then, private theaters charged higher prices than the amphitheaters, probably sixpence, as opposed to a penny for the cheapest entry.

Protected from the weather, the indoor theaters presented plays later in the day than the amphitheaters, and used artificial illumination – candles in sconces or candelabra. But candles melt, and need replacing, snuffing, and trimming, and these practical requirements may have been part of the reason the indoor theaters introduced breaks in the performance, the intermission so dear to the heart of theatergoers and to the pocketbooks of theater concessionaires ever since. Whether motivated by the need to tend to the candles or by the entrepreneurs' wishing to sell oranges and liquor, or both, the indoor theaters eventually established the modern convention of the non-continuous performance. In the early modern "private" theater, musical performances apparently filled the intermissions, which in Stuart theater jargon seem to have been called "acts."

At the end of the first decade of the seventeenth century, the distinction between public amphitheaters and private indoor companies ceased. For various cultural, political, and economic reasons, individual companies gained control of both the public, open-air theaters and the indoor ones, and companies mixing adult men and boys took over the formerly "private" theaters. Despite the death of the boys' companies and of their highly innovative theaters (for which such luminous playwrights as Ben Jonson, George Chapman, and John Marston wrote), their playing spaces and conventions had an immense impact on subsequent plays: not merely for the intervals (which stressed the artistic and architectonic importance of "acts"), but also because they introduced political and social satire as a popular dramatic ingredient, even in tragedy, and a wider range of actorly effects, encouraged by their more intimate playing spaces.

Even the briefest sketch of the Shakespearean theatrical world would be incomplete without some comment on the social and cultural dimensions of theaters and playing in the period. In an intensely hierarchical and status-conscious society, professional actors and their ventures had hardly any respectability; as we have indicated, to protect themselves against laws designed to curb vagabondage and the increase of masterless men, actors resorted to the near-fiction that they were the servants of noble masters, and wore their distinctive livery. Hence the company for which Shakespeare wrote in the 1590s called itself the Lord Chamberlain's Men and pretended that the public, money-getting performances were in fact rehearsals for private performances before that high court official. From 1598, the Privy Council had licensed theatrical companies, and after 1603, with the accession of King James I, the companies gained explicit royal protection, just as the Queen's Men had for a time under Queen Elizabeth. The Chamberlain's Men became the King's Men, and the other companies were patronized by the other members of the royal family.

These designations were legal fictions that half-concealed an important economic and social development, the evolution away from the theater's organization on the model of the guild, a self-regulating confraternity of individual artisans, into a proto-capitalist organization. Shakespeare's company became a joint-stock company, where persons who supplied capital and, in some cases, such as Shakespeare's, capital and talent, employed themselves and others in earning a return on that capital. This development meant that actors and theater companies were outside both the traditional guild structures, which required some form of civic or royal charter, and the feudal household organization of master-and-servant. This anomalous, maverick social and economic condition made theater companies practically unruly and potentially even dangerous; consequently, numerous official bodies – including the London metropolitan and ecclesiastical authorities as well as, occasionally, the royal court itself – tried, without much success, to control and even to disband them.

Public officials had good reason to want to close the theaters: they were attractive nuisances – they drew often riotous crowds, they were always noisy, and they could be politically offensive and socially insubordinate. Until the Civil War, however, anti-theatrical forces failed to shut down professional theater, for many reasons – limited surveillance and few police powers, tensions or outright hostilities among the agencies that sought to check or channel theatrical activity, and lack of clear policies for control. Another reason must have been the theaters' undeniable popularity. Curtailing any activity enjoyed by such a substantial percentage of the population was difficult, as various Roman emperors attempting to limit circuses had learned, and the Tudor-Stuart audience was not merely large, it was socially diverse and included women. The prevalence of public entertainment in this period has been underestimated. In fact, fairs, holidays, games, sporting events, the equivalent of modern parades, freak shows, and street exhibitions all abounded, but the theater was the most widely and frequently available entertainment to which people of every class had access. That fact helps account both for its quantity and for the fear and anger it aroused.

William Shakespeare of Stratford-upon-Avon, Gentleman

Many people have said that we know very little about William Shakespeare's life – pinheads and postcards are often mentioned as appropriately tiny surfaces on which to record the available information. More imaginatively and perhaps more correctly, Ralph Waldo Emerson wrote, "Shakespeare is the only biographer of Shakespeare. . . . So far from Shakespeare's being the least known, he is the one person in all modern history fully known to us."

In fact, we know more about Shakespeare's life than we do about almost any other English writer's of his era. His last will and testament (dated March 25, 1616) survives, as do numerous legal contracts and court documents involving Shakespeare as principal or witness, and parish records in Stratford and London. Shakespeare appears quite often in official records of King James's royal court, and of course Shakespeare's name appears on numerous title pages and in the written and recorded words of his literary contemporaries Robert Greene, Henry Chettle, Francis Meres, John Davies of Hereford, Ben Jonson, and many others. Indeed, if we make due allowance for the bloating of modern, run-of-the-mill bureaucratic records, more information has survived over the past four hundred years about William Shakespeare of Stratford-upon-Avon, Warwickshire, than is likely to survive in the next four hundred years about any reader of these words.

What we do not have are entire categories of information – Shakespeare's private letters or diaries, drafts and revisions of poems and plays, critical prefaces or essays, commendatory verse for other writers' works, or instructions guiding his fellow actors in their performances, for instance – that we imagine would help us understand and appreciate his surviving writings. For all we know, many such data never existed as written records. Many literary and theatrical critics, not knowing what might once have existed, more or less cheerfully accept the situation; some even make a theoretical virtue of it by claiming that such data are irrelevant to understanding and interpreting the plays and poems.

So, what do we know about William Shakespeare, the man responsible for thirty-seven or perhaps more plays, more than 150 sonnets, two lengthy narrative poems, and some shorter poems?

While many families by the name of Shakespeare (or some variant spelling) can be identified in the English Midlands as far back as the twelfth century, it seems likely that the dramatist's grandfather, Richard, moved to Snitterfield, a town not far from Stratford-upon-Avon, sometime before 1529. In Snitterfield, Richard Shakespeare leased farmland from the very wealthy Robert Arden. By 1552, Richard's son John had moved to a large house on Henley Street in Stratford-upon-Avon, the house that stands today as "The Birthplace." In Stratford, John Shakespeare traded as a glover, dealt in wool, and lent money at interest; he also served in a variety of civic posts, including "High Bailiff," the municipality's equivalent of mayor. In 1557, he married Robert Arden's youngest daughter, Mary. Mary and John had four sons – William was the oldest – and four daughters, of whom only Joan outlived her most celebrated sibling. William was baptized (an event entered in the Stratford parish church records) on April 26, 1564, and it has become customary, without any good factual support, to suppose he was born on April 23, which happens to be the feast day of Saint George, patron saint of England, and is also the date on which he died, in 1616. Shakespeare married Anne Hathaway in 1582, when he was eighteen and she was twenty-six; their first child was born five months later. It has been generally assumed that the marriage was enforced and subsequently unhappy, but these are only assumptions; it has been estimated, for instance, that up to one third of Elizabethan brides were pregnant when they married. Anne and William Shakespeare had three children: Susanna, who married a prominent local physician, John Hall; and the twins Hamnet, who died young in 1596, and Judith, who married Thomas Quiney – apparently a rather shady individual. The name Hamnet was unusual but not unique: he and his twin sister were named for their godparents, Shakespeare's neighbors Hamnet and Judith Sadler. Shakespeare's father died in 1601 (the year of *Hamlet*), and Mary Arden Shakespeare died in 1608 (the year of *Coriolanus*). William Shakespeare's last surviving direct descendant was his granddaughter Elizabeth Hall, who died in 1670.

Between the birth of the twins in 1585 and a clear reference to Shakespeare as a practicing London dramatist in Robert Greene's sensationalizing, satiric pamphlet, *Greene's Groatsworth of Wit* (1592), there is no record of where William Shakespeare was or what he was doing. These seven so-called lost years have been imaginatively filled by scholars and other students of Shakespeare: some think he traveled to Italy, or fought in the Low Countries, or studied law or medicine, or worked as an apprentice actor/writer, and so on to even more fanciful possibilities. Whatever the biographical facts for those "lost" years, Greene's nasty remarks in 1592 testify to professional envy and to the fact that Shakespeare already had a successful career in London. Speaking to his fellow playwrights, Greene warns both generally and specifically:

> . . . trust them [actors] not: for there is an upstart crow, beautified with our feathers, that with his tiger's heart wrapped in a player's hide supposes he is as well able to bombast out a blank verse as the best of you; and being an absolute Johannes Factotum, is in his own conceit the only Shake-scene in a country.

The passage mimics a line from *3 Henry VI* (hence the play must have been performed before Greene wrote) and seems to say that "Shake-scene" is both actor and playwright, a jack-of-all-trades. That same year, Henry Chettle protested Greene's remarks in *Kind-Heart's Dream,* and each of the next two years saw the publication of poems – *Venus and Adonis* and *The Rape of Lucrece,* respectively – publicly ascribed to (and dedicated by) Shakespeare. Early in 1595 he was named one of the senior members of a prominent acting company, the Lord Chamberlain's Men, when they received payment for court performances during the 1594 Christmas season.

Clearly, Shakespeare had achieved both success and reputation in London. In 1596, upon Shakespeare's application, the College of Arms granted his father the now-familiar coat of arms he had taken the first steps to obtain almost twenty years before, and in 1598, John's son – now permitted to call himself "gentleman" – took a 10 percent share in the new Globe playhouse. In 1597, he bought a substantial bourgeois house, called New Place, in Stratford – the garden remains, but Shakespeare's house, several times rebuilt, was torn down in 1759 – and over the next few years Shakespeare spent large sums buying land and making other investments in the town and its environs. Though he worked in London, his family remained in Stratford, and he seems always to have considered Stratford the home he would eventually return to. Something approaching a disinterested appreciation of Shakespeare's popular and professional status appears in Francis Meres's *Palladis Tamia* (1598), a not especially imaginative and perhaps therefore persuasive record of literary reputations. Reviewing contemporary English writers, Meres lists the titles of many of Shakespeare's plays, including one not now known, *Love's Labor's Won,* and praises his "mellifluous & hony-tongued" "sugred Sonnets," which were then circulating in manuscript (they were first collected in 1609). Meres describes Shakespeare as "one of the best" English playwrights of both comedy and tragedy. In *Remains . . . Concerning Britain* (1605), William Camden – a more authoritative source than the imitative Meres – calls Shakespeare one of the "most pregnant witts of these our times" and joins him with such writers as Chapman, Daniel, Jonson, Marston, and Spenser. During the first decades of the seventeenth century, publishers began to attribute numerous play quartos, including some non-Shakespearean ones, to Shakespeare, either by name or initials, and we may assume that they deemed Shakespeare's name and supposed authorship, true or false, commercially attractive.

For the next ten years or so, various records show Shakespeare's dual career as playwright and man of the theater in London, and as an important local figure in Stratford. In 1608-9 his acting company – designated the "King's Men" soon after King James had succeeded Queen Elizabeth in 1603 – rented, refurbished, and opened a small interior playing space, the Blackfriars theater, in London, and Shakespeare was once again listed as a substantial sharer in the group of proprietors of the playhouse. By May 11, 1612, however, he describes himself as a Stratford resident in a London lawsuit – an indication that he had withdrawn from day-to-day professional activity and returned to the town where he had always had his main financial interests. When Shakespeare bought a substantial residential building in London, the Blackfriars Gatehouse, close to the theater of the same name, on March 10, 1613, he is recorded as William Shakespeare "of Stratford upon Avon in the county of Warwick, gentleman," and he named several London residents as the building's trustees. Still, he continued to participate in theatrical activity: when the new Earl of Rutland needed an allegorical design to bear as a shield, or *impresa,* at the celebration of King James's Accession Day, March 24, 1613, the earl's accountant recorded a payment of 44 shillings to Shakespeare for the device with its motto.

For the last few years of his life, Shakespeare evidently concentrated his activities in the town of his birth. Most of the final records concern business transactions in Stratford, ending with the notation of his death on April 23, 1616, and burial in Holy Trinity Church, Stratford-upon-Avon.

THE QUESTION OF AUTHORSHIP

The history of ascribing Shakespeare's plays (the poems do not come up so often) to someone else began, as it continues, peculiarly. The earliest published claim that someone else wrote Shakespeare's plays appeared in an 1856 article by Delia Bacon in the American journal *Putnam's Monthly* – although an Englishman, Thomas Wilmot, had shared his doubts in private (even secretive) conversations with friends near the end of the eighteenth century. Bacon's was a sad personal history that ended in madness and poverty, but the year after her article, she published, with great difficulty and the bemused assistance of Nathaniel Hawthorne (then United States Consul in Liverpool, England), her *Philosophy of the Plays of Shakspere Unfolded*. This huge, ornately written, confusing farrago is almost unreadable; sometimes its intents, to say nothing of its arguments, disappear entirely beneath near-raving, ecstatic writing. Tumbled in with much supposed "philosophy" appear the claims that Francis Bacon (from whom Delia Bacon eventually claimed descent), Walter Ralegh, and several other contemporaries of Shakespeare's had written the plays. The book had little impact except as a ridiculed curiosity.

Once proposed, however, the issue gained momentum among people whose conviction was the greater in proportion to their ignorance of sixteenth- and seventeenth-century English literature, history, and society. Another American amateur, Catherine P. Ashmead Windle, made the next influential contribution to the cause when she published *Report to the British Museum* (1882), wherein she promised to open "the Cipher of Francis Bacon," though what she mostly offers, in the words of S. Schoenbaum, is "demented allegorizing." An entire new cottage industry grew from Windle's suggestion that the texts contain hidden, cryptographically discoverable ciphers – "clues" – to their authorship; and today there are not only books devoted to the putative ciphers, but also pamphlets, journals, and newsletters.

Although Baconians have led the pack of those seeking a substitute Shakespeare, in *"Shakespeare" Identified* (1920), J. Thomas Looney became the first published

"Oxfordian" when he proposed Edward de Vere, seventeenth earl of Oxford, as the secret author of Shakespeare's plays. Also for Oxford and his "authorship" there are today dedicated societies, articles, journals, and books. Less popular candidates – Queen Elizabeth and Christopher Marlowe among them – have had adherents, but the movement seems to have divided into two main contending factions, Baconian and Oxfordian. (For further details on all the candidates for "Shakespeare," see S. Schoenbaum, *Shakespeare's Lives,* 2nd ed., 1991.)

The Baconians, the Oxfordians, and supporters of other candidates have one trait in common – they are snobs. Every pro-Bacon or pro-Oxford tract sooner or later claims that the historical William Shakespeare of Stratford-upon-Avon could not have written the plays because he could not have had the training, the university education, the experience, and indeed the imagination or background their author supposedly possessed. Only a learned genius like Bacon or an aristocrat like Oxford could have written such fine plays. (As it happens, lucky male children of the middle class had access to better education than most aristocrats in Elizabethan England – and Oxford was not particularly well educated.) Shakespeare received in the Stratford grammar school a formal education that would daunt many college graduates today; and popular rival playwrights such as the very learned Ben Jonson and George Chapman, both of whom also lacked university training, achieved great artistic success, without being taken as Bacon or Oxford.

Besides snobbery, one other quality characterizes the authorship controversy: lack of evidence. A great deal of testimony from Shakespeare's time shows that Shakespeare wrote Shakespeare's plays and that his contemporaries recognized them as distinctive and distinctly superior. (Some of that contemporary evidence is collected in E. K. Chambers, *William Shakespeare: A Study of Facts and Problems,* 2 vols., 1930.) Since that testimony comes from Shakespeare's enemies and theatrical competitors as well as from his co-workers and from the Elizabethan equivalent of literary journalists, it seems unlikely that, if any of these sources had known he was a fraud, they would have failed to record that fact.

Books About Shakespeare's Theater

Useful scholarly studies of theatrical life in Shakespeare's day include: G. E. Bentley, *The Jacobean and Caroline Stage,* 7 vols. (1941-68), and the same author's *The Professions of Dramatist and Player in Shakespeare's Time, 1590-1642* (1986); E. K. Chambers, *The Elizabethan Stage,* 4 vols. (1923); R. A. Foakes, *Illustrations of the English Stage, 1580-1642* (1985); Andrew Gurr, *The Shakespearean Stage,* 3rd ed. (1992), and the same author's *Play-going in Shakespeare's London,* 2nd ed. (1996); Edwin Nungezer, *A Dictionary of Actors* (1929); Carol Chillington Rutter, ed., *Documents of the Rose Playhouse* (1984).

Books About Shakespeare's Life

The following books provide scholarly, documented accounts of Shakespeare's life: G. E. Bentley, *Shakespeare: A Biographical Handbook* (1961); E. K. Chambers, *William Shakespeare: A Study of Facts and Problems,* 2 vols. (1930); S. Schoenbaum, *William Shakespeare: A Compact Documentary Life* (1977); and *Shakespeare's Lives,* 2nd ed. (1991), by the same author. Many scholarly editions of Shakespeare's complete works print brief compilations of essential dates and events. References to Shakespeare's works up to 1700 are collected in C. M. Ingleby et al., *The Shakespeare Allusion-Book,* rev. ed., 2 vols. (1932).

The Texts of Shakespeare

As far as we know, only one manuscript conceivably in Shakespeare's own hand may (and even this is much disputed) exist: a few pages of a play called *Sir Thomas More*, which apparently was never performed. What we do have, as later readers, performers, scholars, students, are printed texts. The earliest of these survive in two forms: quartos and folios. Quartos (from the Latin for "four") are small books, printed on sheets of paper that were then folded in fours, to make eight double-sided pages. When these were bound together, the result was a squarish, eminently portable volume that sold for the relatively small sum of sixpence (translating in modern terms to about $5.00). In folios, on the other hand, the sheets are folded only once, in half, producing large, impressive volumes taller than they are wide. This was the format for important works of philosophy, science, theology, and literature (the major precedent for a folio Shakespeare was Ben Jonson's *Works,* 1616). The decision to print the works of a popular playwright in folio is an indication of how far up on the social scale the theatrical profession had come during Shakespeare's lifetime. The Shakespeare folio was an expensive book, selling for between fifteen and eighteen shillings, depending on the binding (in modern terms, from about $150 to $180). Twenty Shakespeare plays of the thirty-seven that survive first appeared in quarto, seventeen of which appeared during Shakespeare's lifetime; the rest of the plays are found only in folio.

The First Folio was published in 1623, seven years after Shakespeare's death, and was authorized by his fellow actors, the co-owners of the King's Men. This publication was certainly a mark of the company's enormous respect for Shakespeare; but it was also a way of turning the old plays, most of which were no longer current in the play-house, into ready money (the folio includes only Shake-speare's plays, not his sonnets or other nondramatic verse). Whatever the motives behind the publication of the folio, the texts it preserves constitute the basis for almost all later editions of the playwright's works. The texts, however, dif-fer from those of the earlier quartos, sometimes in minor respects but often significantly – most strikingly in the two texts of *King Lear,* but also in important ways in *Hamlet, Othello,* and *Troilus and Cressida.* (The variants are recorded in the textual notes to each play in the new Pelican series.) The differences in these texts represent, in a sense, the essence of theater: the texts of plays were ini-tially not intended for publication. They were scripts, de-signed for the actors to perform – the principal life of the play at this period was in performance. And it follows that in Shakespeare's theater the playwright typically had no say either in how his play was performed or in the disposi-tion of his text – he was an employee of the company. The authoritative figures in the theatrical enterprise were the shareholders in the company, who were for the most part the major actors. They decided what plays were to be done; they hired the playwright and often gave him an outline of the play they wanted him to write. Often, too, the play was a collaboration: the company would retain a group of writers, and parcel out the scenes among them. The resulting script was then the property of the com-pany, and the actors would revise it as they saw fit during the course of putting it on stage. The resulting text be-longed to the company. The playwright had no rights in it once he had been paid. (This system survives largely intact in the movie industry, and most of the playwrights of Shakespeare's time were as anonymous as most screenwrit-ers are today.) The script could also, of course, continue to change as the tastes of audiences and the requirements of the actors changed. Many – perhaps most – plays were re-vised when they were reintroduced after any substantial absence from the repertory, or when they were performed by a company different from the one that originally commissioned the play.

Shakespeare was an exceptional figure in this world because he was not only a shareholder and actor in his company, but also its leading playwright – he was literally his own boss. He had, moreover, little interest in the publication of his plays, and even those that appeared during his lifetime with the authorization of the company show no signs of any editorial concern on the part of the author. Theater was, for Shakespeare, a fluid and supremely responsive medium – the very opposite of the great classic canonical text that has embodied his works since 1623.

The very fluidity of the original texts, however, has meant that Shakespeare has always had to be edited. Here is an example of how problematic the editorial project inevitably is, a passage from the most famous speech in *Romeo and Juliet,* Juliet's balcony soliloquy beginning "O Romeo, Romeo, wherefore art thou Romeo?" Since the eighteenth century, the standard modern text has read,

> What's Montague? It is nor hand, nor foot,
> Nor arm, nor face, nor any other part
> Belonging to a man. O be some other name!
> What's in a name? That which we call a rose
> By any other name would smell as sweet.
> (II.2.40-44)

Editors have three early texts of this play to work from, two quarto texts and the folio. Here is how the First Quarto (1597) reads:

> Whats *Mountague?* It is nor hand nor foote,
> Nor arme, nor face, nor any other part.
> Whats in a name? That which we call a Rofe,
> By any other name would fmell as fweet:

Here is the Second Quarto (1599):

> Whats *Mountague?* it is nor hand nor foote,
> Nor arme nor face, ô be fome other name
> Belonging to a man.
> Whats in a name that which we call a rofe,
> By any other word would fmell as fweete,

And here is the First Folio (1623):

> What's *Mountague?* it is nor hand nor foote,
> Nor arme, nor face, O be fome other name
> Belonging to a man.
> What? in a names that which we call a Rofe,
> By any other word would fmell as fweete,

There is in fact no early text that reads as our modern text does – and this is the most famous speech in the play. Instead, we have three quite different texts, all of which are clearly some version of the same speech, but none of which seems to us a final or satisfactory version. The transcendently beautiful passage in modern editions is an editorial invention: editors have succeeded in conflating and revising the three versions into something we recognize as great poetry. Is this what Shakespeare "really" wrote? Who can say? What we can say is that Shakespeare always had performance, not a book, in mind.

Books About the Shakespeare Texts

The standard study of the printing history of the First Folio is W. W. Greg, *The Shakespeare First Folio* (1955). J. K. Walton, *The Quarto Copy for the First Folio of Shakespeare* (1971), is a useful survey of the relation of the quartos to the folio. The second edition of Charlton Hinman's *Norton Facsimile* of the First Folio (1996), with a new introduction by Peter Blayney, is indispensable. Stanley Wells, Gary Taylor, John Jowett, and William Montgomery, *William Shakespeare: A Textual Companion,* keyed to the Oxford text, gives a comprehensive survey of the editorial situation for all the plays and poems.

THE GENERAL EDITORS

Introduction

JULIUS CAESAR IS A PLAY about people who make mistakes – costly ones, for themselves and their country. No one in the drama is immune to misreading, misrecognition, and miscalculation, although certain characters, of course, err more gravely than others do. In that the fate of Republican Rome hangs in the balance at the beginning of the play, the stakes are high for everyone involved. If we are inclined to see the political and personal as separate realms, as is often the case in Shakespeare's comedies, in *Julius Caesar* politics *are* personal. Perhaps for this very reason, it is often difficult for the central figures in the play to get their bearings straight; Julius Caesar and Marcus Brutus, for example, both decide upon courses of action and then change their minds. At times, what motivates and dictates the choices that are made is unclear, and indeed at the conclusion of the play – one of Shakespeare's shortest – we might still be inclined to puzzle over the extent to which quick decisions have such calamitous results: Caesar's sudden dismissal of his wife's concerns for his safety, for instance, a seemingly unmotivated change of heart that leads directly to his death; or Brutus's insistence that the conspirators need not fear Mark Antony, the play's ultimate hero, as his triumvirate is victorious at the end.

Julius Caesar may well have been the first play performed by the Lord Chamberlain's Men, Shakespeare's company, in the Globe theater in the early summer of 1599. We cannot be entirely sure. Thomas Platter, a Swiss doctor visiting London in late September of that year, reports seeing the play "very pleasingly performed." Francis Meres's list of plays, included in his *Palladis Tamia: Wits Treasury,* was published in late 1598 and makes no mention of *Julius Caesar*. These two dates have given scholars termini between which it is assumed the play was first performed. Internal evidence in *Henry V*, to be discussed below, situates that play more firmly in the late spring of 1599, just prior to when we believe the Globe to have been completed. Imagining *Henry V* on the Globe's stage before *Caesar* allows us to place *Hamlet* (1601) on the heels of the Roman tragedy, which makes better sense of at least one of the throwaway lines in *Hamlet*: Polonius's reference to having once played Caesar in a university production. If we speculate, as have some scholars, that the same actor assumed both parts for the Lord Chamberlain's Men, then we can appreciate the ways in which a voracious playgoing public (by some estimates, more than 15,000 people attended performances each week, this in a city whose population was roughly 200,000 in 1600) might have shared an inside joke with the actors.

Although it would become, over time, the most renowned theatrical space in the English-speaking world, the construction of the Globe was actually a rush job. Originally the company's financier, James Burbage – father of Shakespeare's friend Richard, the most celebrated actor of his generation and leading man in the company – wanted the troupe to play in London and invested in a theater for that purpose, the second Blackfriars. Residents in and around the site objected, however, and petitioned the Privy Council, which concurred in their reservations. For two years, from 1596 to 1598, the Lord Chamberlain's Men had to rent facilities from other companies to perform, until they had the clever idea of dismantling Burbage's first playhouse, the Theatre, and rebuilding it as the Globe on the Bankside of London in a part of town called the Liberties. Although within the city walls, the Liberties were not, technically speaking, under the jurisdiction of London authorities. Thus, it was an appealing place for entertainers to set up shop, and they did so in great numbers – not only acting companies but also bearbaiters, jugglers, street performers of all stripes, and of course less scrupulous segments of the population: pickpockets, prostitutes, and the like. When thunder and lightning strike at the outset of the third scene of *Julius Caesar,* the noise and tumult constitute the very sort of loud special effects that made residents of London prefer looking at the playhouses from the other side of the Thames.

Why would the Lord Chamberlain's Men have opened the Globe with *Julius Caesar*? Why pursue, in other words, the story of Roman rebellion at the end of Elizabeth's reign? It made sense, in the context of the Earl of Essex's simmering dissatisfaction with Elizabeth's rule (dissatisfaction that Shakespeare might well have heard of from Henry Wriothesley, the third earl of Southampton, a close friend of Essex and a patron of the playwright), for Shakespeare to be drawn to a story about conspiracy, but the very topicality of potential civil unrest made it risky to dwell too much on the subject. Roman history and classical references in general were often deployed in the period to obfuscate contemporary allusions, if only thinly. Caesar, Brutus, and Cassius, as well as Antony and Cleopatra, were enticing figures to the Renaissance both in England and on the European continent precisely because they permitted writers a context in which to explore questions that might otherwise remain taboo: how, in the case of Cleopatra, for example, might sexual obsession compromise a ruler such as Antony, or – more to the point here – was Caesar's fall from power an example of justice served, as some maintained, or regicide?

Queen Elizabeth was by now in her late sixties; her life span had more than doubled the average by 1599. Since she was clearly approaching her demise, and had no children, the question of a successor naturally arose. King James VI of Scotland – the son of Elizabeth's distant cousin Mary, Queen of Scots – would eventually assume the English crown, but not before one failed uprising, the ill-fated rebellion led by Robert Devereux, second earl of Essex, in February of 1601. In the summer of 1599 Essex was in Ireland, leading English forces in an attempt to quell the perpetual Irish rebellion. The prologue to Act Five of *Henry V,* probably finished in the spring, likens the return of a victorious Essex to the arrival of Caesar in Rome, and can be read, in fact, as a rough draft of the opening scene of Shakespeare's Roman play:

> But now behold,
> In the quick forge and working-house of thought,
> How London doth pour out her citizens!
> The mayor and all his brethren in best sort,
> Like to the senators of th' antique Rome,
> With the plebeians swarming at their heels,
> Go forth and fetch their conquering Caesar in;
> As, by a lower but by loving likelihood,
> Were now the general of our gracious empress,
> As in good time he may, from Ireland coming,
> Bringing rebellion broachèd on his sword,
> How many would the peaceful city quit
> To welcome him!
>
> *Henry V,* V. Chorus, 22-34

Imagining Essex's arrival in London, Shakespeare evokes Caesar's successful return after suppressing the uprising of the sons of Pompey, whose forces he subdued in Spain in March of 45 B.C., exactly a year before the events related in *Julius Caesar.* Essex's mission, however – unlike Caesar's – ended in failure. In the winter of 1600, disobeying the queen's orders, Essex returned and was promptly put under house arrest, accused of having dithered on the battlefield and faulted for negotiating an unapproved truce with the enemy, the Celtic leader Hugh O'Neill, Earl of Tyrone.

Beyond the topical appropriateness, and amenability, of Roman history to late Elizabethan English drama and politics, Shakespeare might have been drawn to the idea of inaugurating the Globe with a Roman play out of a desire to unite a specifically theatrical history with public entertainment. English playhouses such as the Globe, the

Rose, the Swan, and the original Theatre were all based upon the model of the classical Roman amphitheater. At times this design drew criticism, as when one preacher at Saint Paul's derisively referred to the playhouse buildings as constructed "after the man[n]er of the olde heathnish Theatre at Rome." For the enterprising playwright and his company, however, it might have seemed fitting to usher in a new Roman playhouse with a new Roman play.

As *Henry V* indicates, Shakespeare has Caesar in mind when he imagines a figure both enigmatic and reckless, such as Essex, returning from a military expedition. And indeed, *Julius Caesar* not only tells the story of the end of an era at the very point in which the Elizabethan era is winding to a close, but also marks a dramaturgical shift on Shakespeare's own part, inaugurating the composition of his mature tragedies. In the 1590s Shakespeare is working out a variety of generic modes that interpenetrate one another. *The Merchant of Venice* (1596) and *Much Ado About Nothing* (1598) have tragic elements, while large portions of *Romeo and Juliet* (1594) and *1 Henry IV* (1596) are deeply comic. *Julius Caesar,* by contrast, begins a period in which Shakespeare's creative energies are more clearly devoted to tragedy. After the first scene, in which a cobbler exasperates the tribunes Flavius and Murellus by punning on the meaning of "soles" and "souls," there is little humor in the play. Neither are there any significant love plots, although the older married couples we encounter are vividly drawn. Calpurnia, for example, deals frankly with her husband in terms that suggest full-grown intimacy rather than the youthful flirtation we typically find in the comedies: "Your wisdom is consumed in confidence," she warns Caesar before he is persuaded by Decius to go to the Senate (II.2.49). Portia is similarly protective of her husband, Brutus, but where Caesar and Calpurnia seem to share completely their lives with each other – her name is the first word uttered by Caesar in the play, and we see them together both in public and private settings – Brutus seems, by contrast, emotionally distanced from his wife, suggesting that his obsession with honor and patriotism has emptied him of a capacity to connect emotionally with others. When he confides to Cassius that his wife is dead, having swallowed fire, Brutus curtails discussion of his loss with a curt "Speak no more of her" (IV.2.210). His coldness adds another twist to our assessment of his putative moral uprightness, while marital love is – at least by the fourth act – entirely removed from the drama.

In the first decade of the 1600s most of Shakespeare's energy would be devoted to tragedies; he would pen seven – nine if we count *Troilus and Cressida* and *Cymbeline,* two generically ambiguous plays included among the tragedies by the compilers of the First Folio (1623). In many ways, *Julius Caesar* establishes the concerns and dilemmas that would prevail in these works. Some readers might have been inclined, for example, to see in Brutus's musings on duty and honor – musings that a Renaissance audience would have understood to be quintessentially Roman – an anticipation of Hamlet's self-absorption, although we might say, to point out but one difference, that Brutus disregards his family for what he conceives as his obligation to serve the best interests of the Roman state, while Hamlet sees in his failure to revenge his father's murder a consequent failure to resuscitate a sick body politic. In this light, the ghost of the unvanquishable ruler Caesar becomes, in *Hamlet,* the paternal ghost to whom the son owes filial and civic obligation. Thus, before Shakespeare composes the great tragedies of familial and monarchical disintegration *Hamlet, Macbeth,* and *King Lear* – he considers, in *Julius Caesar,* a more abstract question in the speculative domain invited by a Roman setting: what constitutes just or unjust political leadership, and with it, honorable or dishonorable service to the state?

Julius Caesar is the second of Shakespeare's four Roman tragedies. The first, *Titus Andronicus* (c. 1593), concerns itself with late Imperial Rome (fourth century): the victory of the Romans over the Goths and the accompanying revenge of the Roman general Titus after his family has been destroyed by the machinations of the foreign Queen Tamora and her sons. The last, *Coriolanus* (1607-8), depicts the rise and fall of the warrior Caius Martius Coriolanus in early Republican Rome (late fifth century B.C.). Coriolanus feels the consulship is owed to him for his various military exploits and thus refuses to grovel before the Roman populace – which he loathes – in order to seize power. More comfortable expressing himself in bloody deeds than in eloquent speeches, the general turns against Rome, laying siege to the city before being slain. *Antony and Cleopatra* (1606-7) turns to the inauguration of Imperial Rome with the passionate love of Mark Antony for Cleopatra and their ensuing defeat at the Battle of Alexandria in 30 B.C. Central to this drama is the disintegration of the second Roman triumvirate, of Antony, Octavius Caesar, and Aemilius Lepidus – the triumvirate that we see triumphant in the Battle of Philippi (42 B.C.) at the conclusion of *Julius Caesar.*

Although the historical context of *Antony and Cleopatra* is set by the events detailed in *Julius Caesar,* Shakespeare's Roman plays are quite clearly *not* a tetralogy; the playwright does not move through Roman history chronologically, and none of the plays makes the kinds of gestures we see at the end of a history play such as *Richard III* (1593-94), when the Earl of Richmond's victory offers at least the hope of a purer and reinvigorated English monarchy. Rather, what distinguishes *Caesar* and *Antony* as plays, as well as such tragedies as *Hamlet, Macbeth,* and *Lear,* is not how we as audience members or readers are to imagine the future, but rather how we might understand a recent, traumatic past.

In its very relation to its historical subject matter, *Caesar* is unique among Shakespeare's plays. Never before has he relied so heavily on one source – in this case, Thomas North's 1579 translation of Jacques Amyot's 1559 French version of a Latin translation of Plutarch's *Lives of the Noble Grecians and Romans.* When current historians and literary scholars who work on the early modern period speak of the recovery of classical texts – a recovery brought about largely by the work of so-called humanists, well-educated men and women with passionate interests in Roman and Greek writings – Plutarch's *Lives* is a principal text that they have in mind. Written in Greek in A.D. 2, the *Lives* offers succinct essays on the accomplishments and experiences of prominent figures from the classical world. The study of Plutarch and Herodotus, along with the Roman writers Seneca, Tacitus, and Livy, encouraged early modern writers to resuscitate literary forms such as the essay. Michel de Montaigne (1533-1592), the most celebrated practitioner of the genre and author of the *Essays* (a work with which Shakespeare displays more than passing familiarity), names Plutarch and Seneca as his favorite authors. For dramatists and poets, on the other hand, Plutarch in particular provided precious information about the prominent personages of the very civilizations that were in the process of being apotheosized by Renaissance thinkers.

While most of the characters and key events in *Coriolanus* and *Antony and Cleopatra* would also derive from Plutarch, Shakespeare's use of the *Lives* in *Julius Caesar* is of a different magnitude. At certain junctures, the playwright turns North's prose directly into iambic pentameter, barely changing a word. At other times, Shakespeare adds features not in Plutarch's original: Caesar's deafness – richly suggestive of vulnerability and arrogance – is Shakespeare's invention, as is nearly all of the Roman crowd's fickleness and volatility. While the alternative settings of Egypt and Rome permit the passage of time to remain largely unacknowledged in *Antony and Cleopatra,* in *Julius Caesar* Shakespeare revises historical chronology by greatly compressing events. Caesar's triumph over Pompey's sons, celebrated in Rome in October 45 B.C., is combined by Shakespeare with the Feast of Lupercal (the traditional celebration of the founding of Rome, held in February) and together these events are shifted to the day before the fateful ides of March. Likewise, Octavius's arrival in Rome, which according to Plutarch occurred many weeks after Caesar's assassination, in Shakespeare takes place the very day of the ruler's death, followed by the rapid, offstage organization of the triumvirate of Antony, Octavius, and Lepidus, an alliance that actually took more than a year to come together.

In that his proximity to his source is so immediate, Shakespeare's departures from Plutarch grasp our attention, and provide us with a wonderful opportunity to gauge his dramatic and thematic aims. To take one telling example, at the conclusion of the third act an angry mob of Romans surrounds an innocent man, named Cinna, and drags him out of sight, to be branded and torn apart. In Plutarch, Cinna the poet is genuinely mistaken for Cinna the conspirator. His death speaks to the dangerous chaos that ensues following Caesar's death. In Shakespeare's play, by contrast, the correct identity is established, but then ignored:

> THIRD PLEBEIAN   Your name, sir, truly.
> CINNA   Truly, my name is Cinna –
> FIRST PLEBEIAN   Tear him to pieces! He's a conspirator.
> CINNA   I am Cinna the *poet!* I am Cinna the *poet!*
> FOURTH PLEBEIAN   Tear him for his bad verses, tear him for his bad verses.
> CINNA   I am not Cinna the conspirator!
> FOURTH PLEBEIAN   It is no matter, his name's Cinna. Pluck but his name out of his heart, and turn him going.
>
> (III.3.26-35)

Even as it plays upon a dark joke (a poet being ripped apart quite literally by a hostile public), the moment is one of the grimmest in all of Shakespeare; far more cynically than Plutarch, the English playwright assumes that it is not merely confusion but unmitigated and needless cruelty that follows a violent change in power. If we are searching for a way of charting Shakespeare's political views in the play, we confront ambiguities and nuances in the portraits of Caesar and Brutus; but we see in Cinna's demise a depiction of the palpable dangers that social chaos unleashes, and the potential victims of such chaos – not only leaders and their families but even poets.

Why, we might ask, is the Globe's inaugural play entitled *Julius Caesar* rather than *Marcus Brutus*? Caesar, after all, dies early in the third act, while Brutus is the figure whose death draws the play to a close. In dramatic terms, the play's title calls attention to the fact that killing Caesar does not dispose of him; he continues to control and direct the energies of the play, even appearing as a ghost before the final battle. In terms of circulating the collective energies of the drama under the name of Caesar, Shakespeare and his company would have tapped into tremendous contemporary interest, and contestation, concerning the Roman general and consul; for – as in the play – the ambiguous aura cast by Caesar resisted any uniform explanation by Elizabethan historians. This ambiguity can be traced back to Roman times. Cicero, though praising Caesar's military accomplishments, defended the assassination, while Plutarch suggested that he was "mortally hated" by the Roman people because of "the covetous desire he had to be called king." In his *Arte of English Poesie* (1589), George Puttenham termed Caesar a "noble Captaine" and "the greatest of Emperours," citing his rumored – although unsubstantiated – dabbling in verse as evidence of the relevance of poetry to the political world. Philip Sidney, in *The Defence of Poesie* (c. 1583), remarks that Caesar's name, "after 1,600 years, lasteth in the highest honor." Other accounts, however, emphasized Caesar's tyrannical inclinations. Thomas Kyd's English translation of the French play *Cornélie* (1594) depicted a despotic Caesar, if not at the beginning of his career then certainly by its end, while – like many humanists – Montaigne was in awe of Roman civilization, and Caesar's abilities as a military leader, but was left frustrated by what was generally perceived to be his greatest weakness:

> This passion of ambition ruled all the others so sovereignly in him [Caesar] and possessed his soul with such full authority that it carried him away where it willed . . . this single vice . . . ruined in him the finest and richest nature that ever was, and has made his memory abominable to all good men, because he willed to seek his glory in the ruin of his country and the subversion of the most powerful and flourishing republic that the world will ever see.*

Caesar's name was, in early modern England, often shorthand for the accomplishments of Roman civilization, and the failings of a singularly talented, if egomaniacal and ambitious, leader. In the sixteenth century, the shadow cast by Rome in the English imagination was enormous. After all, roads first laid out by Roman conquerors were still in use. William Camden's *Britannia* (1586) related – in Latin no less – the history of Roman Britain beginning with Caesar's invasion of the island. The book had gone through five editions by 1600. Before Camden, the English humanist Thomas Starkey had argued – unsuccessfully – that English common law should be replaced by Roman civil law. These were attempts made by increasingly learned, self-conscious Englishmen to detach their culture from its native roots and reattach it to the achievements of classical Rome. And indeed, analogously, Virgil's *Aeneid,* held up by Renaissance poets as the greatest epic poem, had – in the first century B.C. – sought to celebrate Roman culture by tracing the Latin lineage back to the Greeks.

Caesar's influence on the Renaissance was not limited to the strictly political. He had shaped the daily lives of

---

* Michel de Montaigne, *The Complete Essays,* trans. by Donald Frame (Stanford, Calif.: Stanford University Press, 1965), pp. 552, 554.

all Europeans, in fact, through his reformation of the calendar. According to Plutarch, this adjustment – which
included the addition of a number of days to several
months, and the establishment of what came to be known
as a "leap" year every fourth year – drew sharp criticism
from those who saw such intervention as an intrusion
upon the natural order of the cosmos. Elizabethan England would have been sensitive to such issues. In 1582,
when Shakespeare was eighteen, a papal decree corrected
the Julian calendar by adding several days. The English
did not choose to follow suit. The Vatican had already ex-
communicated the Protestant Queen Elizabeth; for England to have accepted the calendrical revision would
have been to acknowledge that the Roman Catholic
Church could dictate the order of the ceremonial, legal,
and social year, something few English Protestants would
have been inclined to admit. The results were, by 1599,
noticeable. Holy days in England were occurring weeks
before they were celebrated in Catholic countries. Adher-
ence to a Julian calendar, unchanged since Caesar's time,
pushed England temporally further and further from the
continent. Thus, when Flavius begins the play by asking
"Is this a holiday?" (I.1.2), or when Brutus requests that
his servant Lucius help him in establishing the date
(II.1.42), their lines emphasize the indeterminate nature
of time as it was experienced both by Roman citizens and,
after them, English subjects. That the decision on the part
of the conspirators to proceed with the assassination attempt is marked by a clock striking three (II.1.192) has
been taken by some commentators to be an anachronistic
lapse on the part of the playwright. But Shakespeare is not
striving for historical verisimilitude. His aims are in fact
far greater than that, for he wants his audience to understand that Caesar not only set the time for his age but for
the Elizabethan age as well. By so doing, he establishes
that Roman civilization does not precede so much as set a
pattern for future epochs; he makes the "Roman" concerns of his play – temporal and political – coterminous

with the present-day concerns of a country that is itself about to change both leadership and centuries.

Caesar's larger-than-life persona not only adjusts the orbit of the planets but the very ways in which other characters in the play understand themselves. As the chief conspirator, Caius Cassius is consumed with jealousy of Caesar; and yet, the latter's imprint on Rome is so great that Cassius feels conspired against by forces that are too massive in his imagination to be located in a single human being. Refusing to recognize the strengths of his nemesis, Cassius instead criticizes the city in which he lives for adding to the luster of Caesar's reputation: "What trash is Rome, / What rubbish, and what offal, when it serves / For the base matter to illuminate / So vile a thing as Caesar!" (I.3.107-10). Cassius is a classic malcontent, a figure frequently seen on the Elizabethan and Jacobean stage. Typically young men whose ambitions have been thwarted, malcontents plot against others out of a sense of being overlooked or merely because of devilish inclinations. Iago, in *Othello,* is perhaps the most memorable of such types in the Shakespearean corpus, and Cassius anticipates Iago's persona in the way he works through others to attain what he wants. His first action in the play is to pull the Soothsayer from the crowd with the command "look upon Caesar" (I.2.23), and indeed he cannot stop himself from obsessing over the general and trying to see him from different perspectives. In an effort to convince Brutus that Caesar is a mere mortal, Cassius tells a story of being challenged by the general to swim across the Tiber (I.2.102-17). Caesar, it turned out, was not such a good swimmer after all, and had Cassius not rescued him he would have drowned. Plutarch tells a very different aquatic story when he describes Caesar, in the midst of a battle, swimming between enemy boats, holding aloft several books in one hand while the Egyptians shoot arrows at him. The former anecdote, by contrast, depicts Caesar in a moment of weakness, but it also reveals Cassius's own sense of inferiority, as well as his great ambition; he wants to replace the godlike Caesar with himself.

Cassius, of course, is mistaken; Caesar is not a mere mortal. He might have once struggled to stay afloat, but he has since risen far above his contemporaries in prestige and power. And yet, Cassius's very desire to do away with Caesar makes him more like the play's namesake than anyone else. Like Caesar, he is a shrewd judge of others. "[H]onor," he assures Brutus before describing his exploits in the Tiber, "is the subject of my story" (I.2.94). On the contrary, honor has no bearing on Cassius's actions; it is a mere word that can be manipulated for any ends whatsoever, and yet Cassius knows how much such words mean to Brutus, who loves the "name of honor" more than he fears death (I.2.91). Cassius's ability to read others is noted by none other than Caesar. "He reads much," the general comments to Antony. "He is a great observer, and he looks / Quite through the deeds of men" (I.2.202-4). It is precisely by focusing on Brutus's idealism that Cassius manipulates the praetor (a high-ranking magistrate) against Caesar; he notes after his first encounter with Brutus,

> Well, Brutus, thou art noble; yet I see
> Thy honorable mettle may be wrought
> From that it is disposed. Therefore it is meet
> That noble minds keep ever with their likes;
> For who so firm that cannot be seduced?
> (I.2.307-11)

Left vulnerable to Cassius's deviousness, Brutus's mind is not equipped to defend itself. He is too smug, in fact, too assured that because he is "so strong in honesty" nothing can corrupt him (IV.2.122).

Overconfident that his ideals can be relied upon regardless of external circumstances or the perfidiousness of others, Brutus makes several strategic blunders leading up to and following the assassination of Caesar. Cassius's

errors follow closely behind, for by yielding to Brutus's
opinions rather than following his own, he seals the fate
of their rebellion. Brutus first underestimates Mark
Antony, insisting that the conspirators spare his life and
then permitting him to deliver a funeral oration that
quickly stirs the Roman populace against the conspirators. "Antony is but a limb of Caesar," Brutus insists.
"[T]hink not of him, / For he can do no more than Caesar's arm / When Caesar's head is off" (II.1.165, 181-83).
Cassius disagrees, rightly fearing "the engrafted love he
[Antony] bears to Caesar" (184), but he nonetheless con-
cedes, perhaps suspecting that his inherent animosity
toward the Roman citizenry makes him a poor evaluator
of their sentiments. When Brutus agrees to permit Mark
Antony to speak to the crowds, Cassius's judgment again
proves to be more accurate: "You know not what you do.
Do not consent / That Antony speak in his funeral. /
Know you how much the people may be moved / By that
which he will utter?" (III.1.234-37). Much later, as the
forces of Antony's triumvirate grow, Brutus insists upon
an aggressive battle strategy that ultimately proves disas-
trous. Here too Cassius expresses reservations: "'Tis better
that the enemy seek us," he insists. "So shall he waste his
means, weary his soldiers, / Doing himself offense; whilst
we, lying still, / Are full of rest, defense, and nimbleness"
(IV.2.251-54). Later, after the Battle of Philippi has
begun, Brutus errs again, permitting his soldiers to seize
spoils while their allies are surrounded by Antony's troops
(V.3.5-8). Through Brutus's persistent miscalculations we
see a rather cynical assessment on the part of Shakespeare
of the capabilities of the intellectual in the world of politics and action. Hamlet will make these characteristics
significantly more telling, finding himself metaphysically
bound in a nutshell while he remains incapable of trust-
ing the ghost of his father or the culpability of his uncle
without greater and greater proof. In *Julius Caesar,* one
man of principles – Brutus – is compromised by a man of
ruthless cunning and manipulation – Cassius – and yet

Brutus ends by compromising Cassius's effectiveness as well. They are, in tragic terms, the perfect tandem. _couple_

Scholars have often noted that Brutus is more idealistic and less ambitious in Shakespeare than in Plutarch, but to suggest that, as a result, Shakespeare is easier on him is to miss the playwright's more subtle point about the particular dangers posed by idealism. In the most extended glimpse we have of a solitary Brutus, when he is alone in his garden contemplating whether or not to rise up against Caesar, we find him cornered by the very hypotheticals his mind so effortlessly produces:

> to speak truth of Caesar,
> I have not known when his affections swayed
> More than his reason. But 'tis a common proof
> That lowliness is young ambition's ladder,
> Whereto the climber-upward turns his face;
> But when he once attains the upmost round,
> He then unto the ladder turns his back,
> Looks in the clouds, scorning the base degrees
> By which he did ascend.
>
> (II.1.19-27)

The most important decision of Brutus's life is shaped by a conditional. Attention to personality and disposition, which both Caesar and Cassius reveal as foundational for their approaches to others, is here dismissed. Although the Renaissance view of Brutus was generally favorable, Shakespeare could have followed more critical commentators, such as Dante, who placed both Brutus and Cassius in the deepest circle of his _Inferno._ Caesar errs in some of the ways that Cassius does – for example, by listening to the wrong people, especially Decius Brutus, who preys on the general's weakness for flattery by convincing him that avoiding the Senate might doom his chances of obtaining the crown (II.2.92-104). Caesar's mistakes are fateful, but Brutus's errors are perhaps more pitiable; he is the only conspirator with the introspectiveness required to be tor-

Brutus is the only conspirator who worries about his conscience

mented by his conscience, represented by the ghost of Caesar. His life, as Antony notes at the play's conclusion, was "gentle," too gentle for the business in which it became embroiled (V.5.72).

Like Brutus, Antony commits a glaring error early in the play, dismissing Caesar's wary assessment of Cassius (I.2.197–98). Antony, however, recovers from this blunder. Why, we might ask, is he the only character in the play able to redeem himself after making a mistake? The answer, it seems, has much to do with his attitude toward Caesar's legacy. Where Cassius envies, and Brutus speculates, Antony relishes; he does not step back from the shadow cast by Caesar so much as luxuriate in it, strengthening himself in the process. In his only soliloquy, immediately following the assassination, Antony addresses Caesar's body, asking for strength: "Over thy wounds now do I prophesy. . . . To beg the voice and utterance of my tongue" (III.1.262–64). While Brutus imagines power emanating from one's convictions, and Cassius sees manipulation as the key to acquiring political dominion, Antony understands that it is through rhetoric, the art of persuasion, that he can garner the support of the Roman citizenry, and with this support the reins of power. Where Brutus underestimates the populace, and Cassius resents it, Antony appeals to it. He is the most public of all the characters we encounter in the play, and his funeral elegy – among the most famous speeches in English drama – succeeds precisely because of the way it first seizes on, and then builds upon, one of the most striking props in all of Shakespeare: Caesar's corpse.

Unaware of the power of what we would today call "spin control," Brutus speaks before Antony, appealing to his own "honor" so as to defend the murder of Caesar. Antony, by contrast, does not ask his audience to grant him any virtues whatsoever. He does not, of course, "come to bury Caesar," as he suggests (III.2.74). Rather, he summons Caesar's ghost long before the spirit appears to Brutus. Entering with Caesar's body in tow, Antony proceeds to juxtapose this physical reminder of brutal violence with the increasingly meaningless category of Brutus's elusive "honor." Brutus "is an honorable man," we hear again and again (III.2.82, 87, 94, 99), but each time the term loses that much more resonance. How, Antony asks implicitly, is Brutus's honor to replace the slain Caesar when it is nowhere to be seen? Where Brutus speaks in scrupulous prose, overlooking the importance of style out of a principled concern for rational explication, Antony's words are delivered in measured pentameter, punctuated by emotional halts that the line breaks enforce: "Bear with me. / My heart is in the coffin there with Caesar, / And I must pause till it come back to me" (III.2.105-7). Rather than minimize Caesar's greatness, as did Cassius when he described him drowning, Antony celebrates it, ending his speech where it began, as a meditation on the violence done to the "noble Caesar" (III.2.181). When he returns to the word "honorable," Antony associates it with the sphere of "private griefs," a realm that the citizens have learned – by this point in the oration – to distrust, for it is out of their eyesight, in secret, that the conspiracy was planned and Caesar was slain (III.2.207, 208). Having taken a very "public leave" to praise the murdered Roman, Antony raises himself in the eyes of the people by lowering himself in relation to Caesar (III.2.214). His eventual victory is one predicated on the understanding that a base of support is built on verbal inducement, not on the mere justification of one's actions.

The protagonist of Shakespeare's last Roman play, Coriolanus, is banished from Rome because he refuses to ingratiate himself with its citizenry. His unwillingness to recount his military exploits – and thus permit the Roman populace to experience his sufferings communally – results in his expulsion. Antony, by contrast, speaks through the wounds of Caesar. His victory, secured with Octavius and Lepidus, is a victory for those who guard the legacy of a powerful ruler – one with faults, but one inarguably touched by greatness. In early modern England, this message of continuity and remembrance appears to have reverberated strongly; *Julius Caesar* was performed again and again through the seventeenth century, into and beyond the reign of Elizabeth's successor, King James I. In 1599, the play would have served as a timely reminder of the enormous upheaval that could follow an attempt to seize power through violent means. And yet, there is no single figure on whom the label of usurper can fall. By depriving Caesar of the crown, the conspirators might have spared Rome from prolonged, autocratic rule. By defeating the conspirators, Antony and his allies appear to have righted the wrongs committed by an envious band of oligarchs. But righted these wrongs for whom? The fact that Antony succeeds in bringing the populace to his side does not necessarily mean that he has the people's best interests in mind, only that he has persuaded them to his point of view most effectively. *Julius Caesar* does not permit its audience to find easy comfort in any of its conclusions. Brutus, a man of unquestioned virtue, lies dead at the end, while Caesar's legacy is carried on by committee, through a triumvirate that will itself crumble in less than a decade. *Julius Caesar* clearly rejects conspiracy, but the play's attitudes toward the threat of autocracy, or even the viability of republicanism, are less apparent. That such questions are permitted to linger speaks to the unique indeterminacy allowed by the genre of the Roman play in Shakespeare's hands. What is not at all ambiguous is that *Julius Caesar* secured the place of the Lord Chamberlain's Men (soon to be the King's Men) as the preeminent players in Renaissance London, with a new theater to call their home, and a growing repertoire of plays – foremost among them, in the early 1600s, tragedies – that are among the most compelling and remarkable artistic achievements of early modern Europe.

DOUGLAS TREVOR
University of Iowa

Note on the Text

THE EARLIEST, and also the only authorative, text of *Julius Caesar* – the one from which all later editions derive, including this one – is the one printed in the 1623 first edition, *Mr William Shakespeares Comedies, Histories, and Tragedies,* generally known as the First Folio (F1 or simply F). This text is exceptionally cleanly printed, but close examination of it over the past couple of decades powerfully suggests that there was some revision to the manuscript from which the printed text was set.

Much of this work was done by John Jowett as he prepared his edition of the play for the Oxford *Complete Works* (1986). I am persuaded by his arguments in the *Textual Companion to Shakespeare* (1986) and elsewhere, and in general my text closely follows his.

This edition silently regularizes speech prefixes, expands stage directions where this appears necessary, and modernizes all spelling. Act and scene divisions, erratic in the folio, are here made on the basis of a stage cleared of all characters. All substantive emendations apart from these exceptions are recorded below; the adopted reading is in italics, followed by the folio reading in roman.

I.2 104 *Said Caesar* Caesar saide   140 *were* are   156 *walls* Walkes
I.3 128 *In favor's* Is Fauors
II.1 40 *ides* first   67 *of* of a   83 *put* path   96 *Cinna, this* this, Cinna   266 *his* hit   312 *LIGARIUS* Cai.   315 *LIGARIUS* Cai.   319 *LIGARIUS* Cai.   327 *LIGARIUS* Cai.   330 *LIGARIUS* Cai.
II.2 46 *are* heare   81 *Of* And   108 *Cassius* Publius   109 *CASSIUS* Pub.   109 *Cassius* Publius
III.1 39 *law* lane   47 *but with just cause* not in F   114 *states* State   116 *lies* lye   175 *unstrung* in strength   286 *for* from
III.2 49 *FOURTH PLEBEIAN* 2. (The Second Plebeian is among those who leave to hear Cassius speak. His speeches have been assigned throughout the rest of this scene to the Fourth Plebeian. Likewise, the speeches F assigns to the Fourth Plebeian are for the rest of this scene reassigned to the Fifth

Plebeian; see the next note.)   50 *FIFTH PLEBEIAN* 4.   104 *art* are   110 *he not* hee   198–99 *revenged . . . Revenge!* reueng'd: Reuenge   215 *wit* writ
IV.1 44 *meinies* meanes
IV.2 2 *SOLDIER* Lucil.   34 *FIRST SOLDIER* not in F   35 *SECOND SOLDIER* not in F   36 *THIRD SOLDIER* not in F   170 *ill-tempered too.* ill remper'd too.s   204 *Impatience* Impatient   271 *to* ro   301 *will* will it
V.1 42 *teeth* teethes   55 *swords* Sword   79 *ensigns* Ensigne   88 *give* giue up   95 *rest* rests
V.3 103 *Thasos* Tharsus   107 *Labeo* Labio; *Flavius* Flauio
V.4 7 *LUCILLIUS* not in F
V.5 23 **s.d.** *Low* An earlier state of F reads "Loud"   76 *With all* Withall

The Tragedy of
Julius Caesar

NAMES OF THE ACTORS

JULIUS CAESAR
CALPURNIA, *his wife*

Joint rulers of Rome after Caesar's death
MARC ANTONY
OCTAVIUS, *Caesar's adopted son*
LEPIDUS

*Conspirators against Caesar, and their families, servants,
and supporters*
MARCUS BRUTUS, *a Roman patrician*
CAIUS CASSIUS
CASCA
CINNA
DECIUS BRUTUS } *the conspirators*
CAIUS LIGARIUS
METELLUS CIMBER
TREBONIUS

PORTIA, *Brutus's wife*

CLAUDIO
CLITUS
DARDANIUS
FLAVIUS *(nonspeaking)*
LABEO *(nonspeaking)* } *officers or servants to Brutus*
LUCIUS
STRATO
VARRUS

PINDARUS, *Cassius's servant*

YOUNG CATO
LUCILLIUS
MESSALA   } *friends of Brutus*
STATILLIUS *(nonspeaking)*   *and Cassius*
TITINIUS
VOLUMNIUS

Tribunes of the people of Rome
FLAVIUS
MURELLUS

Senators of Rome
CICERO
POPILLIUS LAENA
PUBLIUS

Others
A SOOTHSAYER
ARTEMIDORUS, *a doctor of rhetoric*
CINNA, *a poet*
ANOTHER POET
A CARPENTER
A COBBLER
A MESSENGER, PLEBEIANS, SENATORS, SERVANTS,
    SOLDIERS

SCENE: *Rome; near Sardis; near Philippi*
*

The Tragedy of Julius Caesar

❧ **I.1** *Enter Flavius, Murellus, and certain Commoners over the stage.*

FLAVIUS
Hence, home, you idle creatures, get you home!
Is this a holiday? What, know you not,
Being mechanical, you ought not walk   3
Upon a laboring day without the sign   4
Of your profession? *(To one of the Commoners)* Speak,
what trade art thou?

CARPENTER   Why, sir, a carpenter.

MURELLUS
Where is thy leather apron and thy rule?
What dost thou with thy best apparel on?
    To another of the Commoners
You, sir, what trade are you?

COBBLER   Truly, sir, in respect of a fine workman I am   10
but, as you would say, a cobbler.   11

MURELLUS
But what trade art thou? Answer me directly.   12

COBBLER   A trade, sir, that I hope I may use with a safe
conscience, which is indeed, sir, a mender of bad soles.   14

I.1 A street in Rome **s.d.** *over the stage* who cross the stage before halting
3 *mechanical* workers   4 *sign* tools and costume (which indicate a man's
trade)   10 *in . . . workman* as far as skilled work is concerned   11 *cobbler*
(with pun on "bungler")   12 *directly* plainly   14 *soles* (with pun on "souls")

FLAVIUS

15 What trade, thou knave? Thou naughty knave, what
trade?

16 COBBLER   Nay, I beseech you, sir, be not out with me. Yet
17 if you be out, sir, I can mend you.

MURELLUS

What mean'st thou by that? Mend me, thou saucy fellow?

COBBLER   Why, sir, cobble you.

20 FLAVIUS   Thou art a cobbler, art thou?

COBBLER   Truly, sir, all that I live by is with the awl. I
22 meddle with no tradesman's matters, nor women's mat-
23 ters, but withal I am indeed, sir, a surgeon to old shoes:
24 when they are in great danger I recover them. As proper
25 men as ever trod upon neat's leather have gone upon
my handiwork.

FLAVIUS

But wherefore art not in thy shop today?
Why dost thou lead these men about the streets?

COBBLER   Truly, sir, to wear out their shoes to get myself
30 into more work. But indeed, sir, we make holiday to see
31 Caesar, and to rejoice in his triumph.

MURELLUS

Wherefore rejoice? What conquest brings he home?
33 What tributaries follow him to Rome
34 To grace in captive bonds his chariot wheels?
35 You blocks, you stones, you worse than senseless things!
O, you hard hearts, you cruel men of Rome,
37 Knew you not Pompey? Many a time and oft
Have you climbed up to walls and battlements,
To towers and windows, yea to chimney tops,

---

15 *naughty* wicked   16 *out* angry   17 *be out* (1) be angry, (2) have worn-out
shoes; *mend* (with pun on "reform")   22 *meddle* (with pun on "am intimate")   22–23 *women's matters* (with pun on "genitals")   23 *withal* neverthe-
less (with puns on *all* and *awl*)   24 *recover* re-sole (with pun on "cure");
proper fine   25 *neat's* cattle's; *gone* walked   31 *triumph* victory procession
33 *tributaries* ransom-paying captives   34 *chariot wheels* (to which captives
were tied)   35 *senseless* inanimate   37 *Pompey* (defeated Caesar in 48 B.C.;
later murdered)

Your infants in your arms, and there have sat   40
The livelong day with patient expectation
To see great Pompey pass the streets of Rome.
And when you saw his chariot but appear,
Have you not made an universal shout,
That Tiber trembled underneath her banks   45
To hear the replication of your sounds   46
Made in her concave shores?   47
And do you now put on your best attire?
And do you now cull out a holiday?   49
And do you now strew flowers in his way   50
That comes in triumph over Pompey's blood?   51
Be gone!
Run to your houses, fall upon your knees,
Pray to the gods to intermit the plague   54
That needs must light on this ingratitude.

FLAVIUS
Go, go, good countrymen, and for this fault
Assemble all the poor men of your sort;   57
Draw them to Tiber banks, and weep your tears
Into the channel, till the lowest stream
Do kiss the most exalted shores of all.   60

                              Exeunt all the Commoners.
See whe'er their basest mettle be not moved.   61
They vanish tongue-tied in their guiltiness.
Go you down that way towards the Capitol;
This way will I. Disrobe the images   64
If you do find them decked with ceremonies.   65

MURELLUS
May we do so?
You know it is the Feast of Lupercal.   67

---

45 *That* such that   46 *replication* echo   47 *concave shores* hollowed-out
banks   49 *cull out* choose   51 *blood* offspring (also the blood of Pompey
and his followers)   54 *intermit* withhold   57 *sort* rank   60 *most exalted
shores* (1) highest flood level, (2) verge of heavens   61 *whe'er* whether; *their
basest* even their very best; *mettle* (1) substance, (2) temperament   64 *images*
statues   65 *ceremonies* ornaments   67 *Feast of Lupercal* fertility festival (held
on February 15)

FLAVIUS
    It is no matter. Let no images
69   Be hung with Caesar's trophies. I'll about,
70   And drive away the vulgar from the streets;
    So do you too where you perceive them thick.
    These growing feathers plucked from Caesar's wing
73   Will make him fly an ordinary pitch,
74   Who else would soar above the view of men
    And keep us all in servile fearfulness.   *Exeunt.*

*

∾ **I.2** *Loud music. Enter Caesar, Antony stripped for the*
course, Calpurnia, Portia, Decius, Cicero, Brutus,
Cassius, Casca, a Soothsayer, a throng of Citizens;
after them, Murellus and Flavius.

CAESAR
    Calpurnia.
CASCA
    Peace, ho! Caesar speaks.
    Music ceases.
CAESAR
    Calpurnia.
CALPURNIA
    Here, my lord.
CAESAR
    Stand you directly in Antonio's way
6   When he doth run his course. Antonio.
ANTONY
    Caesar, my lord.
CAESAR
    Forget not in your speed, Antonio,
    To touch Calpurnia, for our elders say

---

69 *trophies* ornaments **70** *vulgar* plebeians, common people **73** *an ordinary pitch* medium height (image from falconry) **74** *else* otherwise; *above . . . men* i.e., like the gods
    I.2 A public place in Rome **6** *run his course* i.e., race naked through the city striking bystanders with a goatskin thong

The barren, touchèd in this holy chase,   *10*
Shake off their sterile curse.
ANTONY   I shall remember:
When Caesar says "Do this," it is performed.
CAESAR
Set on, and leave no ceremony out.   13
    Music.
SOOTHSAYER
Caesar!
CAESAR
Ha! Who calls?
CASCA
Bid every noise be still. Peace yet again.
    Music ceases.
CAESAR
Who is it in the press that calls on me?   17
I hear a tongue shriller than all the music
Cry "Caesar!" Speak. Caesar is turned to hear.
SOOTHSAYER
Beware the ides of March.   20
CAESAR   What man is that?
BRUTUS
A soothsayer bids you beware the ides of March.
CAESAR
Set him before me; let me see his face.
CASSIUS
Fellow, come from the throng; look upon Caesar.
    The Soothsayer comes forward.
CAESAR
What sayst thou to me now? Speak once again.
SOOTHSAYER
Beware the ides of March.
CAESAR
He is a dreamer. Let us leave him. Pass!   26

---

13 *Set on* proceed   **17** *press* crowd   **20** *ides* the halfway point in the month
(the fifteenth day in March, May, July, and October)   **26** *Pass* proceed; **s.d.**
Sennet trumpet call

*Sennet. Exeunt all but
Brutus and Cassius.*

CASSIUS
27   Will you go see the order of the course?
BRUTUS
    Not I.
CASSIUS
    I pray you, do.
BRUTUS
30   I am not gamesome; I do lack some part
31   Of that quick spirit that is in Antony.
    Let me not hinder, Cassius, your desires.
    I'll leave you.
CASSIUS
    Brutus, I do observe you now of late.
35   I have not from your eyes that gentleness
36   And show of love as I was wont to have.
37   You bear too stubborn and too strange a hand
    Over your friend that loves you.
BRUTUS   Cassius,
39   Be not deceived. If I have veiled my look,
40   I turn the trouble of my countenance
41   Merely upon myself. Vexèd I am
42   Of late with passions of some difference,
43   Conceptions only proper to myself,
44   Which give some soil, perhaps, to my behaviors.
    But let not therefore my good friends be grieved –
    Among which number, Cassius, be you one –
47   Nor construe any further my neglect

---

27 *order of the course* running of the race   30 *gamesome* sports-loving   31 *quick spirit* lively nature   35 *gentleness* well-bred politeness   36 *love* friendship; *wont* accustomed   37 *strange* unfriendly; *a hand* (the allusion is to horse handling)   37–38 *bear . . . Over* behave roughly and unnaturally to   39 *veiled my look* i.e., concealed my true friendship   40 *trouble of my countenance* my troubled appearance   41 *Merely* wholly   42 *passions . . . difference* conflicting emotions   43 *proper to* concerning   44 *soil* blemish   47 *construe* interpret

Than that poor Brutus, with himself at war,
Forgets the shows of love to other men.   49

CASSIUS
Then, Brutus, I have much mistook your passion,   50
By means whereof this breast of mine hath buried   51
Thoughts of great value, worthy cogitations.
Tell me, good Brutus, can you see your face?

BRUTUS
No, Cassius, for the eye sees not itself
But by reflection, by some other things.

CASSIUS
'Tis just;   56
And it is very much lamented, Brutus,
That you have no such mirrors as will turn   58
Your hidden worthiness into your eye,   59
That you might see your shadow. I have heard   60
Where many of the best respect in Rome –   61
Except immortal Caesar – speaking of Brutus,
And groaning underneath this age's yoke,
Have wished that noble Brutus had his eyes.   64

BRUTUS
Into what dangers would you lead me, Cassius,
That you would have me seek into myself
For that which is not in me?

CASSIUS
Therefor, good Brutus, be prepared to hear.   68
And since you know you cannot see yourself
So well as by reflection, I, your glass,   70
Will modestly discover to yourself   71
That of yourself which you yet know not of.
And be not jealous on me, gentle Brutus.   73

---

49 *shows* manifestations **50** *passion* feelings **51** *By means whereof* i.e., and
as a result of this mistake; *buried* concealed **56** *just* true **58** *turn* reflect
59 *hidden worthiness* true nobility, inner worth **60** *shadow* reflection **61**
best respect highest repute **64** *Brutus had his eyes* (so that he could see prop-
erly) **68** *Therefor* as to that **70** *glass* mirror **71** *modestly* without exagger-
ation; *discover* reveal **73** *jealous on* suspicious of

74 Were I a common laughter, or did use
75 To stale with ordinary oaths my love
76 To every new protester; if you know
That I do fawn on men and hug them hard,
78 And after scandal them; or if you know
79 That I profess myself in banqueting
80 To all the rout: then hold me dangerous.
     Flourish and shout within.

BRUTUS
What means this shouting? I do fear the people
Choose Caesar for their king.

CASSIUS   Ay, do you fear it?
Then must I think you would not have it so.

BRUTUS
I would not, Cassius; yet I love him well.
But wherefore do you hold me here so long?
What is it that you would impart to me?
87 If it be aught toward the general good,
Set honor in one eye and death i' th' other,
89 And I will look on both indifferently;
90 For let the gods so speed me as I love
The name of honor more than I fear death.

CASSIUS
I know that virtue to be in you, Brutus,
93 As well as I do know your outward favor.
Well, honor is the subject of my story.
I cannot tell what you and other men
96 Think of this life; but for my single self,
97 I had as lief not be, as live to be
98 In awe of such a thing as I myself.

---

74 *laughter* object of ridicule; *did use* were accustomed   75 *stale* cheapen; *ordinary* tavern (?), commonplace (?)   76 *protester* one who easily declares friendship   78 *scandal* slander   79 *profess myself* declare my friendship   80 *rout* rabble; **s.d.** *Flourish* elaborate trumpet call   87 *general good* welfare of the state   89 *indifferently* impartially   90 *speed me* make me prosper; *as* to the extent that   93 *favor* appearance   96 *single* particular   97 *as lief . . . as* rather . . . than   98 *such . . . myself* i.e., a mere mortal

I was born free as Caesar, so were you.
We both have fed as well, and we can both   *100*
Endure the winter's cold as well as he.
For once upon a raw and gusty day,
The troubled Tiber chafing with her shores,   103
Said Caesar to me "Dar'st thou, Cassius, now
Leap in with me into this angry flood,
And swim to yonder point?" Upon the word,   106
Accoutred as I was I plungèd in,   107
And bade him follow. So indeed he did.
The torrent roared, and we did buffet it
With lusty sinews, throwing it aside,   *110*
And stemming it with hearts of controversy.   111
But ere we could arrive the point proposed,   112
Caesar cried "Help me, Cassius, or I sink!"
Ay, as Aeneas our great ancestor   114
Did from the flames of Troy upon his shoulder
The old Anchises bear, so from the waves of Tiber
Did I the tirèd Caesar. And this man
Is now become a god, and Cassius is
A wretched creature, and must bend his body   119
If Caesar carelessly but nod on him.   *120*
He had a fever when he was in Spain,
And when the fit was on him, I did mark
How he did shake. 'Tis true, this god did shake.
His coward lips did from their color fly;   124
And that same eye whose bend doth awe the world   125
Did lose his luster. I did hear him groan,   126
Ay, and that tongue of his that bade the Romans

---

103 *chafing with* raging against   106 *point* promontory   107 *Accoutred* i.e.,
fully armed   111 *stemming . . . controversy* making headway with keen com-
petition   112 *arrive* attain   114–16 *Aeneas . . . Anchises* (Virgil relates how
the Trojan hero Aeneas, rescuing his father, Anchises, from burning Troy,
went on to found the Roman nation. The story became a familiar example of
filial devotion.)   119 *bend* bow   124 *His . . . fly* he turned pale (i.e., the
color fled from his lips like cowardly soldiers deserting their flag)   125 *bend*
glance   126 *his* its

Mark him and write his speeches in their books,
"Alas!" it cried, "Give me some drink, Titinius,"
130   As a sick girl. Ye gods, it doth amaze me
131   A man of such a feeble temper should
132   So get the start of the majestic world,
133   And bear the palm alone!
          Flourish and shout within.
BRUTUS   Another general shout!
       I do believe that these applauses are
       For some new honors that are heaped on Caesar.
CASSIUS
       Why, man, he doth bestride the narrow world
137   Like a Colossus, and we petty men
       Walk under his huge legs, and peep about
       To find ourselves dishonorable graves.
140   Men at sometime were masters of their fates.
       The fault, dear Brutus, is not in our stars,
       But in ourselves, that we are underlings.
       Brutus and Caesar: what should be in that "Caesar"?
144   Why should that name be sounded more than yours?
       Write them together: yours is as fair a name.
       Sound them: it doth become the mouth as well.
       Weigh them: it is as heavy. Conjure with 'em:
148   "Brutus" will start a spirit as soon as "Caesar."
       Now in the names of all the gods at once,
150   Upon what meat doth this our Caesar feed
       That he is grown so great? Age, thou art shamed.
       Rome, thou hast lost the breed of noble bloods.
153   When went there by an age since the great flood,
154   But it was famed with more than with one man?
       When could they say till now, that talked of Rome,

---

131 *temper* constitution   **132** *get the start of* outstrip all others in   **133** *palm* victor's prize   **137** *Colossus* gigantic statue (famously straddling the harbor at Rhodes); *petty* inconsiderable   **140** *at sometime* formerly   **144** *sounded* pronounced (with pun on "proclaimed")   **148** *start* raise up (like a god's name) **150** *meat* food   **153** *flood* Deucalion's flood (the classical version of a great annihilating inundation, like those of Noah and Gilgamesh)   **154** *famed with* renowned for

That her wide walls encompassed but one man?
Now is it Rome indeed, and room enough   157
When there is in it but one only man.
O, you and I have heard our fathers say
There was a Brutus once that would have brooked   160
Th' eternal devil to keep his state in Rome   161
As easily as a king.

BRUTUS
That you do love me I am nothing jealous.   163
What you would work me to I have some aim.   164
How I have thought of this and of these times
I shall recount hereafter. For this present,   166
I would not, so with love I might entreat you,   167
Be any further moved. What you have said   168
I will consider. What you have to say
I will with patience hear, and find a time   170
Both meet to hear and answer such high things.   171
Till then, my noble friend, chew upon this: 172
Brutus had rather be a villager
Than to repute himself a son of Rome
Under these hard conditions as this time   175
Is like to lay upon us.

CASSIUS   I am glad
That my weak words have struck but thus much show
Of fire from Brutus.   178
          Music. Enter Caesar and his train.

BRUTUS
The games are done, and Caesar is returning.

CASSIUS
As they pass by, pluck Casca by the sleeve,   180

---

157 *room* (pronounced like *Rome*)   160 *a Brutus* (Lucius Junius Brutus: one
of the founders of the Roman Republic in 509 B.C., an ancestor of Marcus
Brutus and famous for expelling Rome's royal family, the Tarquins, from the
city); *brooked* tolerated   161 *eternal* i.e., eternally damned; *keep his state* hold
court   163 *am nothing jealous* have no doubt   164 *work* persuade; *aim* idea
166 *this present* the present time   167 *so with love* if in friendship   168
moved persuaded   171 *meet* fitting; *high* serious   172 *chew upon* consider
175 *these* such   178 **s.d.** *train* followers

181 And he will, after his sour fashion, tell you
182 What hath proceeded worthy note today.

BRUTUS
    I will do so. But look you, Cassius,
    The angry spot doth glow on Caesar's brow,
    And all the rest look like a chidden train.
    Calpurnia's cheek is pale, and Cicero
187 Looks with such ferret and such fiery eyes
    As we have seen him in the Capitol
189 Being crossed in conference by some senators.

CASSIUS
190 Casca will tell us what the matter is.

CAESAR
    Antonio.

ANTONY
    Caesar.

CAESAR
193 Let me have men about me that are fat,
194 Sleek-headed men, and such as sleep anights.
195 Yon Cassius has a lean and hungry look.
    He thinks too much. Such men are dangerous.

ANTONY
    Fear him not, Caesar, he's not dangerous.
198 He is a noble Roman, and well given.

CAESAR
    Would he were fatter! But I fear him not.
200 Yet if my name were liable to fear,
    I do not know the man I should avoid
    So soon as that spare Cassius. He reads much,
    He is a great observer, and he looks
204 Quite through the deeds of men. He loves no plays,

---

181 *sour* harsh   182 *worthy* worthy of   187 *ferret* like those of a ferret (a weasel-like animal with red, darting eyes)   189 *crossed* opposed; *conference* debate   193 *fat* plump (not "obese")   194 *Sleek-headed* well-groomed   195 *lean* (proverbially associated with envy)   198 *given* disposed   200 *my name . . . to* I were capable of   204 *through . . . men* i.e., to the motivations behind men's actions

As thou dost, Antony; he hears no music.   205
Seldom he smiles, and smiles in such a sort   206
As if he mocked himself, and scorned his spirit
That could be moved to smile at anything.
Such men as he be never at heart's ease
Whiles they behold a greater than themselves,   210
And therefore are they very dangerous.
I rather tell thee what is to be feared
Than what I fear, for always I am Caesar.
Come on my right hand, for this ear is deaf,
And tell me truly what thou think'st of him.
                    Sennet. Exeunt Caesar and his train.
          Brutus, Cassius, and Casca remain.
CASCA   *(To Brutus)* You pulled me by the cloak. Would 216
    you speak with me?
BRUTUS
    Ay, Casca. Tell us what hath chanced today,
    That Caesar looks so sad.   219
CASCA   Why, you were with him, were you not?   220
BRUTUS
    I should not then ask Casca what had chanced.
CASCA   Why, there was a crown offered him; and being
    offered him, he put it by with the back of his hand,
    thus; and then the people fell a-shouting.
BRUTUS   What was the second noise for?
CASCA
    Why, for that too.
CASSIUS
    They shouted thrice. What was the last cry for?
CASCA   Why, for that too.
BRUTUS   Was the crown offered him thrice?

---

205 *hears no music* (see *The Merchant of Venice*, V.1.83–88: "The man that
hath no music in himself . . . Is fit for treasons . . . Let no such man be
trusted") **206** *sort* manner **216** *pulled me by the cloak* i.e., pulled me to one
side **219** *sad* serious

230 CASCA   Ay, marry, was't; and he put it by thrice, every
         time gentler than other; and at every putting by, mine
232   honest neighbors shouted.

CASSIUS
         Who offered him the crown?

CASCA   Why, Antony.

BRUTUS
234   Tell us the manner of it, gentle Casca.

CASCA   I can as well be hanged as tell the manner of it. It
236   was mere foolery, I did not mark it. I saw Mark Antony
         offer him a crown – yet 'twas not a crown neither, 'twas
238   one of these coronets – and as I told you he put it by
239   once; but for all that, to my thinking he would fain
240   have had it. Then he offered it to him again; then he
         put it by again – but to my thinking he was very loath
         to lay his fingers off it. And then he offered it the third
243   time; he put it the third time by. And still as he refused
         it, the rabblement hooted, and clapped their chapped
245   hands, and threw up their sweaty nightcaps, and ut-
         tered such a deal of stinking breath because Caesar re-
         fused the crown that it had almost choked Caesar; for
248   he swooned and fell down at it. And for mine own part,
         I durst not laugh for fear of opening my lips and receiv-
250   ing the bad air.

CASSIUS
251   But soft, I pray you. What, did Caesar swoon?

CASCA   He fell down in the marketplace, and foamed at
         mouth, and was speechless.

BRUTUS
254   'Tis very like: he hath the falling sickness.

CASSIUS
         No, Caesar hath it not; but you and I

---

230 *marry* indeed (originally an oath on the name of the Virgin Mary)   232
honest worthy (ironic)   234 *gentle* noble   236 *mere foolery* totally absurd
238 *coronets* small crowns wreathed with laurel   239 *fain* willingly   243
still continually, each time   245 *nightcaps* i.e., the citizens' caps (contemptuous)   248 *swooned* fainted   251 *soft* slowly   254 *like* likely (Plutarch suggests that Caesar feigned an attack); *falling sickness* epilepsy

And honest Casca, we have the falling sickness.   256

CASCA   I know not what you mean by that, but I am sure
Caesar fell down. If the tagrag people did not clap him   258
and hiss him, according as he pleased and displeased
them, as they use to do the players in the theater, I am   260
no true man.

BRUTUS
What said he when he came unto himself?

CASCA   Marry, before he fell down, when he perceived
the common herd was glad he refused the crown, he
plucked me ope his doublet and offered them his throat   265
to cut. An I had been a man of any occupation, if I   266
would not have taken him at a word, I would I might   267
go to hell among the rogues. And so he fell. When he
came to himself again, he said, if he had done or said
anything amiss, he desired their worships to think it   270
was his infirmity. Three or four wenches where I stood
cried "Alas, good soul!" and forgave him with all their
hearts. But there's no heed to be taken of them: if Caesar had stabbed their mothers they would have done no   274
less.

BRUTUS
And after that he came thus sad away?   276

CASCA   Ay.

CASSIUS   Did Cicero say anything?

CASCA   Ay, he spoke Greek.

CASSIUS   To what effect?   280

CASCA   Nay, an I tell you that, I'll ne'er look you i' th'
face again. But those that understood him smiled at
one another, and shook their heads. But for mine own
part, it was Greek to me. I could tell you more news,
too. Murellus and Flavius, for pulling scarves off Cae-   285

---

256 *we . . . sickness* i.e., we are declining (into subjection)   258 *tagrag people*
riffraff   260 *use* are accustomed   265 *plucked me ope* pulled open; *doublet*
short jacket   266 *An* if; *man . . . occupation* working man (also "man of action"?)   267 *a* his   274 *stabbed* (playing on "sexually penetrate")   276 *sad*
seriously   285 *scarves* (the ornaments, or *ceremonies,* mentioned at I.1.65)

286 sar's images, are put to silence. Fare you well. There was
more foolery yet, if I could remember it.

CASSIUS Will you sup with me tonight, Casca?

289 CASCA No, I am promised forth.

290 CASSIUS Will you dine with me tomorrow?

291 CASCA Ay, if I be alive, and your mind hold, and your
dinner worth the eating.

CASSIUS Good; I will expect you.

CASCA Do so. Farewell both.   *Exit.*

BRUTUS
What a blunt fellow is this grown to be!

296 He was quick mettle when he went to school.

CASSIUS
So is he now, in execution
Of any bold or noble enterprise,

299 However he puts on this tardy form.

300 This rudeness is a sauce to his good wit,

301 Which gives men stomach to digest his words
With better appetite.

BRUTUS
And so it is. For this time I will leave you.
Tomorrow, if you please to speak with me,

305 I will come home to you; or if you will,
Come home to me and I will wait for you.

CASSIUS
307 I will do so. Till then, think of the world. *Exit Brutus.*
Well, Brutus, thou art noble; yet I see

309 Thy honorable mettle may be wrought

310 From that it is disposed. Therefore it is meet
That noble minds keep ever with their likes;

---

286 *put to silence* i.e., deprived of their tribuneships and exiled (the tribunes
were the guardians of the rights of the plebeians) 289 *promised forth* previ-
ously engaged 291 *hold* does not change 296 *quick mettle* of a lively temperament 299 *tardy form* sluggish appearance 300 *rudeness* harshness; *wit*
intellect 301 *stomach* disposition 305 *come home to* visit 307 *the world*
i.e., the times we are experiencing 309–10 *wrought . . . disposed* so worked
upon as to change its natural qualities 310 *meet* fitting

For who so firm that cannot be seduced?
Caesar doth bear me hard, but he loves Brutus.   313
If I were Brutus now, and he were Cassius,
He should not humor me. I will this night   315
In several hands in at his windows throw –   316
As if they came from several citizens –
Writings, all tending to the great opinion   318
That Rome holds of his name, wherein obscurely   319
Caesar's ambition shall be glancèd at.   320
And after this, let Caesar seat him sure,   321
For we will shake him, or worse days endure.   *Exit.*   322

                              *

∾ **I.3** *Thunder and lightning. Enter Casca, at one door,
       with his sword drawn, and Cicero at another.*

CICERO
Good even, Casca. Brought you Caesar home?   1
Why are you breathless, and why stare you so?
CASCA
Are not you moved, when all the sway of earth   3
Shakes like a thing unfirm? O Cicero,
I have seen tempests when the scolding winds
Have rived the knotty oaks, and I have seen   6
Th' ambitious ocean swell and rage and foam
To be exalted with the threat'ning clouds;   8
But never till tonight, never till now,
Did I go through a tempest dropping fire.   10
Either there is a civil strife in heaven,
Or else the world, too saucy with the gods,   12
Incenses them to send destruction.

---

313 *bear me hard* bear a grudge against me   315 *He* i.e., Brutus; *humor* influence   316 *several hands* different handwritings   318 *tending to* intimat-
ing   319 *obscurely* in a roundabout way   320 *glancèd* hinted   321 *him sure*
himself firmly in power   322 *shake him* i.e., from his dominant position
   I.3 A street in Rome   1 *Brought* accompanied   3 *sway* established order
6 *rived* split   8 *exalted with* raised to the level of   12 *saucy* insolent

CICERO

14   Why, saw you anything more wonderful?

CASCA

A common slave – you know him well by sight –
Held up his left hand, which did flame and burn
Like twenty torches joined; and yet his hand,

18   Not sensible of fire, remained unscorched.

19   Besides – I ha' not since put up my sword –

20   Against the Capitol I met a lion

21   Who glazed upon me, and went surly by

22   Without annoying me. And there were drawn

23   Upon a heap a hundred ghastly women,
Transformèd with their fear, who swore they saw
Men all in fire walk up and down the streets.

26   And yesterday the bird of night did sit
Even at noonday upon the marketplace,

28   Hooting and shrieking. When these prodigies

29   Do so conjointly meet, let not men say

30   "These are their reasons," "they are natural,"
For I believe they are portentous things

32   Unto the climate that they point upon.

CICERO

Indeed it is a strange-disposèd time;

34   But men may construe things after their fashion,

35   Clean from the purpose of the things themselves.
Comes Caesar to the Capitol tomorrow?

CASCA

He doth, for he did bid Antonio
Send word to you he would be there tomorrow.

CICERO

Good night then, Casca. This disturbèd sky

---

14 *more* else   18 *sensible of* feeling   19 *put up* sheathed   20 *Against* opposite   21 *glazed* stared   22 *annoying* harming   22–23 *drawn . . . heap*
crowded together   23 *ghastly* ghostlike, pale   26 *bird of night* screech owl
(proverbially ill-omened)   28 *prodigies* abnormal events   29 *conjointly meet*
happen all at the same time   32 *climate* region   34 *construe* interpret; *after
their fashion* each in his own way   35 *Clean . . . purpose* contrary to the
meaning

Is not to walk in.   40
CASCA   Farewell, Cicero.   *Exit Cicero.*
   Enter Cassius, unbraced.
CASSIUS
   Who's there?
CASCA   A Roman.
CASSIUS   Casca, by your voice.
CASCA
   Your ear is good. Cassius, what night is this?
CASSIUS
   A very pleasing night to honest men.
CASCA
   Who ever knew the heavens menace so?
CASSIUS
   Those that have known the earth so full of faults.
   For my part, I have walked about the streets,
   Submitting me unto the perilous night;
   And thus unbracèd, Casca, as you see,
   Have bared my bosom to the thunderstone;   49
   And when the cross blue lightning seemed to open   50
   The breast of heaven, I did present myself
   Even in the aim and very flash of it.   52
CASCA
   But wherefore did you so much tempt the heavens?
   It is the part of men to fear and tremble   54
   When the most mighty gods by tokens send   55
   Such dreadful heralds to astonish us.   56
CASSIUS
   You are dull, Casca, and those sparks of life
   That should be in a Roman you do want,   58
   Or else you use not. You look pale, and gaze,
   And put on fear, and cast yourself in wonder,   60
   To see the strange impatience of the heavens;

---

40 s.d. *unbraced* with doublet unbuttoned (i.e., hurriedly, in a state of un-
readiness) 49 *thunderstone* thunderbolt, lightning 50 *cross* (1) forked, (2)
hostile 52 *Even* exactly 54 *part* appropriate action 55 *tokens* signs 56
heralds precursors; *astonish* terrify 58 *want* lack 60 *put on* manifest;
cast . . . wonder are astonished

But if you would consider the true cause
Why all these fires, why all these gliding ghosts,
64   Why birds and beasts from quality and kind –
65   Why old men, fools, and children calculate –
66   Why all these things change from their ordinance,
67   Their natures, and preformèd faculties,
68   To monstrous quality – why, you shall find
69   That heaven hath infused them with these spirits
70   To make them instruments of fear and warning
71   Unto some monstrous state. Now could I, Casca,
Name to thee a man most like this dreadful night,
That thunders, lightens, opens graves, and roars
As doth the lion in the Capitol;
A man no mightier than thyself or me
76   In personal action, yet prodigious grown,
77   And fearful, as these strange eruptions are.

CASCA
'Tis Caesar that you mean, is it not, Cassius?

CASSIUS
Let it be who it is; for Romans now
80   Have thews and limbs like to their ancestors.
81   But woe the while! Our fathers' minds are dead,
And we are governed with our mothers' spirits.
83   Our yoke and sufferance show us womanish.

CASCA
Indeed they say the senators tomorrow
Mean to establish Caesar as a king,
And he shall wear his crown by sea and land
87   In every place save here in Italy.

CASSIUS   *Drawing his dagger*

---

64 *from . . . kind* contrary to their nature   65 *old men* i.e., in their second childhood; *calculate* compute future events, prophesy   66 *ordinance* established modes of behavior   67 *preformèd faculties* congenital qualities   68 *monstrous* unnatural   69 *spirits* powers (?), demons (?)   71 *monstrous state* (1) abnormal situation, (2) atrocious government   76 *prodigious* ominous   77 *fearful* causing fear, terrifying; *eruptions* upheavals   80 *thews* sinews   81 *woe the while* alas for the times   83 *yoke* servitude; *sufferance* meek endurance   87 *every place* i.e., all parts of the Roman Empire

I know where I will wear this dagger then:
Cassius from bondage will deliver Cassius.
Therein, ye gods, you make the weak most strong;   90
Therein, ye gods, you tyrants do defeat.
Nor stony tower, nor walls of beaten brass,
Nor airless dungeon, nor strong links of iron,
Can be retentive to the strength of spirit;   94
But life, being weary of these worldly bars,   95
Never lacks power to dismiss itself.
If I know this, know all the world besides,   97
That part of tyranny that I do bear
I can shake off at pleasure.   99
     Thunder still.
CASCA   So can I.
So every bondman in his own hand bears   *100*
The power to cancel his captivity.
CASSIUS
And why should Caesar be a tyrant then?
Poor man, I know he would not be a wolf
But that he sees the Romans are but sheep.
He were no lion, were not Romans hinds.   105
Those that with haste will make a mighty fire
Begin it with weak straws. What trash is Rome,
What rubbish, and what offal, when it serves   108
For the base matter to illuminate   109
So vile a thing as Caesar! But, O grief,   *110*
Where hast thou led me? I perhaps speak this
Before a willing bondman; then I know
My answer must be made. But I am armed,   113
And dangers are to me indifferent.   114
CASCA
You speak to Casca, and to such a man

---

90 *Therein* i.e., in suicide   **94** *be retentive to* confine   **95** *bars* hindrances
97 *know all . . . besides* let everyone else know   **99** s.d. *still* continually   **105**
hinds female deer (with a pun on "peasants")   **108** *offal* refuse   **109** *base* (1)
underlying, (2) despicable   **113** *My . . . made* I must pay the penalty; *armed*
i.e., both physically and morally   **114** *indifferent* a matter of indifference

116   That is no fleering telltale. Hold. My hand.
117   Be factious for redress of all these griefs,
        And I will set this foot of mine as far
119   As who goes farthest.
         They join hands.
    CASSIUS   There's a bargain made.
120   Now know you, Casca, I have moved already
        Some certain of the noblest-minded Romans
122   To undergo with me an enterprise
123   Of honorable-dangerous consequence.
124   And I do know by this they stay for me
125   In Pompey's Porch; for now, this fearful night,
        There is no stir or walking in the streets,
127   And the complexion of the element
128   In favor's like the work we have in hand,
        Most bloody, fiery, and most terrible.
         Enter Cinna.
    CASCA
130   Stand close a while, for here comes one in haste.
    CASSIUS
        'Tis Cinna; I do know him by his gait.
        He is a friend. Cinna, where haste you so?
    CINNA
133   To find out you. Who's that? Metellus Cimber?
    CASSIUS
134   No, it is Casca, one incorporate
135   To our attempts. Am I not stayed for, Cinna?
    CINNA
136   I am glad on't. What a fearful night is this!
        There's two or three of us have seen strange sights.

---

116 *fleering* sneering; *Hold* enough   117 *Be factious* form a group   119 *who* whoever   120 *moved* persuaded   122 *undergo* undertake   123 *honorable* honorably   124 *by . . . stay* by this time they are waiting   125 *Pompey's Porch* the colonnade of the theater built by Pompey   127 *complexion . . . element* appearance of the sky   128 *In favor's* in appearance is   130 *close* concealed   133 *find out* look for   134 *incorporate* closely associated   135 *stayed for* awaited   136 *on't* of it

CASSIUS
   Am I not stayed for? Tell me.
CINNA
   Yes, you are.
   O Cassius, if you could   *140*
   But win the noble Brutus to our party –
CASSIUS
   Be you content. Good Cinna, take this paper,
      He gives Cinna letters.
   And look you lay it in the praetor's chair,   143
   Where Brutus may but find it; and throw this   144
   In at his window. Set this up with wax
   Upon old Brutus' statue. All this done,   146
   Repair to Pompey's Porch where you shall find us.
   Is Decius Brutus and Trebonius there?   148
CINNA
   All but Metellus Cimber, and he's gone
   To seek you at your house. Well, I will hie,   150
   And so bestow these papers as you bade me.   151
CASSIUS
   That done, repair to Pompey's Theater.   *Exit Cinna.*   152
   Come, Casca, you and I will yet ere day   153
   See Brutus at his house. Three parts of him   154
   Is ours already, and the man entire
   Upon the next encounter yields him ours.   156
CASCA
   O, he sits high in all the people's hearts,
   And that which would appear offense in us
   His countenance, like richest alchemy,   159

---

143 *praetor's chair* official seat of the chief magistrates (Brutus was one of six-teen of these; see the note to II.4.37)   144 *may but* must surely   146 *old Brutus'* Lucius Junius Brutus's (see the note to I.2.160)   148 *Decius Brutus* a kinsman of Marcus Brutus (his name was really Decimus)   150 *hie* hasten   151 *bestow* distribute   152 *repair* return   153 *ere* before   154 *Three parts* three quarters (?), three of the four physiological humors (?) (see the note to V.5.72)   156 *yields him ours* i.e., will join our faction   159 *countenance* (1) support, (2) appearance; *alchemy* the proto-science devoted to transmuting base metals into gold

160   Will change to virtue and to worthiness.

CASSIUS

    Him and his worth, and our great need of him,

162   You have right well conceited. Let us go,

    For it is after midnight, and ere day

    We will awake him and be sure of him.   *Exeunt.*

               *

  ❧ **II.1**   *Enter Brutus in his orchard.*

BRUTUS   *Calling*

    What, Lucius, ho!

      Aside

    I cannot by the progress of the stars

    Give guess how near to day. *(Calling)* Lucius, I say!

      Aside

    I would it were my fault to sleep so soundly.

      Calling

5   When, Lucius, when? Awake, I say! What, Lucius!

      Enter Lucius.

LUCIUS   Called you, my lord?

BRUTUS

7   Get me a taper in my study, Lucius.

    When it is lighted, come and call me here.

LUCIUS   I will, my lord.   *Exit.*

BRUTUS

10   It must be by his death. And for my part

11   I know no personal cause to spurn at him,

12   But for the general. He would be crowned.

    How that might change his nature, there's the question.

    It is the bright day that brings forth the adder,

15   And that craves wary walking. Crown him: that!

    And then I grant we put a sting in him

---

162 *conceited* conceived (with pun on "expressed in a fanciful simile")

    II.1 Outside Brutus's house **s.d.** *orchard* garden   **5** *When* (exclamation of impatience)   **7** *taper* candle   **10** *his* i.e., Caesar's   **11** *spurn at* kick against **12** *general* (good) – i.e., public welfare, health of the state   **15** *craves* calls for; *Crown him: that* i.e., king (a word Brutus here avoids)

That at his will he may do danger with.   17
Th' abuse of greatness is when it disjoins
Remorse from power. And to speak truth of Caesar,   19
I have not known when his affections swayed   20
More than his reason. But 'tis a common proof   21
That lowliness is young ambition's ladder,   22
Whereto the climber-upward turns his face;
But when he once attains the upmost round,   24
He then unto the ladder turns his back,
Looks in the clouds, scorning the base degrees   26
By which he did ascend. So Caesar may.
Then lest he may, prevent. And since the quarrel   28
Will bear no color for the thing he is,   29
Fashion it thus: that what he is, augmented,   30
Would run to these and these extremities;   31
And therefore think him as a serpent's egg,
Which, hatched, would as his kind grow mischievous,   33
And kill him in the shell.
        Enter Lucius, with a letter.

LUCIUS
    The taper burneth in your closet, sir.   35
    Searching the window for a flint, I found
    This paper, thus sealed up, and I am sure
    It did not lie there when I went to bed.
        He gives him the letter.

BRUTUS
    Get you to bed again; it is not day.
    Is not tomorrow, boy, the ides of March?   40
LUCIUS   I know not, sir.

---

17 *danger* harm   19 *Remorse* mercy   20 *affections swayed* passions ruled   21
common proof commonplace, conventional observation based on experience
22 *lowliness* (apparent) humility   24 *round* rung   26 *base degrees* lower
rungs of the ladder (with pun on "lower grades of office," possibly referring
to the Roman *cursus honorum*)   28 *prevent* takes measures to forestall; *quarrel* case (against Caesar)   29 *bear no color* carry no conviction; *the thing he is*
his conduct up to now (i.e., we cannot possibly justify his murder on the
basis of his actions so far)   30 *Fashion it* put the case   31 *extremities* ex-
tremes (of tyranny)   33 *his kind* by its nature; *mischievous* harmful   35
closet private room

BRUTUS
42   Look in the calendar and bring me word.
LUCIUS   I will, sir.   *Exit.*
BRUTUS
44   The exhalations whizzing in the air
      Give so much light that I may read by them.
        He opens the letter and reads.
      "Brutus, thou sleep'st. Awake, and see thyself.
      Shall Rome, et cetera? Speak, strike, redress." –
      "Brutus, thou sleep'st. Awake."
      Such instigations have been often dropped
50   Where I have took them up.
      "Shall Rome, et cetera?" Thus must I piece it out:
52   Shall Rome stand under one man's awe? What, Rome?
      My ancestors did from the streets of Rome
      The Tarquin drive when he was called a king.
      "Speak, strike, redress." Am I entreated
      To speak and strike? O Rome, I make thee promise,
57   If the redress will follow, thou receivest
58   Thy full petition at the hand of Brutus.
        Enter Lucius.

LUCIUS
59   Sir, March is wasted fifteen days.
        Knock within.
BRUTUS
60   'Tis good. Go to the gate; somebody knocks.
                                Exit Lucius.
61   Since Cassius first did whet me against Caesar
      I have not slept.
      Between the acting of a dreadful thing
64   And the first motion, all the interim is
65   Like a phantasma or a hideous dream.

---

42 *calendar* i.e., the Julian calendar (instituted by Caesar in 46 B.C.)   44 *exhalations* meteors   52 *under . . . awe* in fear of one man   57 *redress* i.e., correction of abuses in the Republic   58 *Thy full petition* all you ask   59 *fifteen* (the Romans counted both the day from which and the day to which they reckoned)   61 *whet* incite   64 *motion* proposal   65 *phantasma* hallucination, nightmare

The genius and the mortal instruments   66
Are then in counsel, and the state of man,   67
Like to a little kingdom, suffers then
The nature of an insurrection.
     Enter Lucius.

LUCIUS
Sir, 'tis your brother Cassius at the door,   70
Who doth desire to see you.
BRUTUS   Is he alone?
LUCIUS
No, sir, there are more with him.
BRUTUS   Do you know them?
LUCIUS
No, sir; their hats are plucked about their ears,
And half their faces buried in their cloaks,
That by no means I may discover them   75
By any mark of favor.   76
BRUTUS   Let 'em enter.   *Exit Lucius.*
They are the faction. O conspiracy,
Sham'st thou to show thy dang'rous brow by night,
When evils are most free? O then by day   79
Where wilt thou find a cavern dark enough   80
To mask thy monstrous visage? Seek none, conspiracy.
Hide it in smiles and affability;
For if thou put thy native semblance on,   83
Not Erebus itself were dim enough   84
To hide thee from prevention.   85
     Enter the Conspirators, muffled: Cassius, Casca,
     Decius, Cinna, Metellus, and Trebonius.

---

66 *genius* guardian spirit; *mortal instruments* intellectual and emotional faculties   **67–69** *the state . . . insurrection* (the analogy was commonly drawn
between the health of a man and that of the body politic)   **70** *brother* i.e.,
brother-in-law (Cassius was married to Brutus's sister, Junia)   **75** *discover*
recognize, identify   **76** *favor* appearance   **79** *evils . . . free* evil things range
abroad most freely   **83** *native semblance* true, natural appearance   **84** *Erebus*
region of primeval darkness between the upper earth and Hades   **85** *prevention* being forestalled

CASSIUS
86   I think we are too bold upon your rest.
      Good morrow, Brutus. Do we trouble you?
BRUTUS
      I have been up this hour, awake all night.
      Know I these men that come along with you?
CASSIUS
90   Yes, every man of them; and no man here
      But honors you; and every one doth wish
      You had but that opinion of yourself
      Which every noble Roman bears of you.
      This is Trebonius.
BRUTUS   He is welcome hither.
CASSIUS
      This, Decius Brutus.
BRUTUS   He is welcome too.
CASSIUS
      This, Casca; Cinna, this; and this, Metellus Cimber.
BRUTUS
      They are all welcome.
98   What watchful cares do interpose themselves
      Betwixt your eyes and night?
CASSIUS   Shall I entreat a word?
        Cassius and Brutus stand aside and whisper.
DECIUS
100   Here lies the east. Doth not the day break here?
CASCA
      No.
CINNA
      O pardon, sir, it doth; and yon gray lines
103   That fret the clouds are messengers of day.
CASCA
      You shall confess that you are both deceived.
        He points his sword.
      Here, as I point my sword, the sun arises,

---

86 *upon* in intruding on   **98** *watchful* sleep-preventing   **103** *fret* ornamen-
tally interlace

Which is a great way growing on the south,   106
Weighing the youthful season of the year.   107
Some two months hence up higher toward the north
He first presents his fire, and the high east   109
Stands, as the Capitol, directly here.   *110*
    He points his sword.
    Brutus and Cassius join the other Conspirators.

BRUTUS
Give me your hands all over, one by one.
    He shakes their hands.

CASSIUS
And let us swear our resolution.

BRUTUS
No, not an oath. If not the face of men,   113
The sufferance of our souls, the time's abuse –   114
If these be motives weak, break off betimes,   115
And every man hence to his idle bed.   116
So let high-sighted tyranny range on   117
Till each man drop by lottery. But if these,   118
As I am sure they do, bear fire enough   119
To kindle cowards and to steel with valor   *120*
The melting spirits of women, then, countrymen,   121
What need we any spur but our own cause   122
To prick us to redress? What other bond   123
Than secret Romans, that have spoke the word   124
And will not palter? And what other oath   125
Than honesty to honesty engaged   126
That this shall be or we will fall for it?
Swear priests and cowards and men cautelous,   128

---

106 *growing on* toward   **107** *Weighing* considering   **109** *high* due, exact
113 *face* (grave) expressions   **114** *sufferance* distress; *time's abuse* corruption
of these days (i.e., Caesar's violation of the laws of the Republic)   **115** *be-*
times at once   **116** *idle* unused   **117** *high-sighted* looking down from on
high (like a falcon – i.e., arrogant)   **118** *lottery* whim; *these* these reasons
119 *fire* i.e., spirit, courage   **121** *melting* yielding   **122** *What* why   **123**
prick spur   **124** *secret Romans* that we are Romans (1) able to hold our
tongues(?), (2) sharing a secret (?); *spoke the word* given one another our word
of honor   **125** *palter* quibble   **126** *honesty* personal honor; *engaged* pledged
128 *Swear* make swear, bind by oath; *cautelous* crafty, deceitful

129 Old feeble carrions, and such suffering souls
130 That welcome wrongs; unto bad causes swear
131 Such creatures as men doubt; but do not stain
132 The even virtue of our enterprise,
133 Nor th' insuppressive mettle of our spirits,
134 To think that or our cause or our performance
Did need an oath, when every drop of blood
That every Roman bears, and nobly bears,
137 Is guilty of a several bastardy
If he do break the smallest particle
Of any promise that hath passed from him.

CASSIUS
140 But what of Cicero? Shall we sound him?
I think he will stand very strong with us.

CASCA
Let us not leave him out.

CINNA   No, by no means.

METELLUS
O, let us have him, for his silver hairs
144 Will purchase us a good opinion,
And buy men's voices to commend our deeds.
It shall be said his judgment ruled our hands.
147 Our youths and wildness shall no whit appear,
148 But all be buried in his gravity.

BRUTUS
149 O, name him not! Let us not break with him,
150 For he will never follow anything
That other men begin.

CASSIUS
Then leave him out.

CASCA
Indeed he is not fit.

---

129 *carrions* physical wrecks, practically corpses   130 *welcome wrongs* gladly submit to oppression   131 *doubt* suspect   132 *even* just, straightforward 133 *insuppressive* indomitable   134 *or . . . or* either . . . or   137 *several* separate, individual   140 *sound him* find out what he thinks   144 *purchase* procure; *opinion* reputation   147 *no whit* not at all   148 *gravity* sobriety and authority of character   149 *break with* disclose our plans to

DECIUS
   Shall no man else be touched, but only Caesar?
CASSIUS
   Decius, well urged. I think it is not meet   155
   Mark Antony, so well beloved of Caesar,
   Should outlive Caesar. We shall find of him   157
   A shrewd contriver. And you know his means,   158
   If he improve them, may well stretch so far   159
   As to annoy us all; which to prevent,   160
   Let Antony and Caesar fall together.
BRUTUS
   Our course will seem too bloody, Caius Cassius,   162
   To cut the head off and then hack the limbs,
   Like wrath in death and envy afterwards –   164
   For Antony is but a limb of Caesar.   165
   Let's be sacrificers, but not butchers, Caius.
   We all stand up against the spirit of Caesar,   167
   And in the spirit of men there is no blood.
   O, that we then could come by Caesar's spirit,   169
   And not dismember Caesar! But, alas,   *170*
   Caesar must bleed for it. And, gentle friends,   171
   Let's kill him boldly, but not wrathfully.
   Let's carve him as a dish fit for the gods,
   Not hew him as a carcass fit for hounds.
   And let our hearts, as subtle masters do,   175
   Stir up their servants to an act of rage,   176
   And after seem to chide 'em. This shall make
   Our purpose necessary, and not envious;   178
   Which so appearing to the common eyes,
   We shall be called purgers, not murderers.   180
   And for Mark Antony, think not of him,

---

155 *urged* recommended; *meet* proper   157 *of* in   158 *shrewd contriver* formidable plotter; *means* capacity (to harm us)   159 *improve* exploit   160 *annoy* injure; *prevent* forestall   162 *course* (punning on "corse," corpse)   164 *envy* malice   165 *limb* mere appendage   167 *spirit* principles (i.e., Caesarism)   169 *come by* get at   171 *gentle* noble   175 *subtle* cunning   176 *servants* i.e., our hands   178 *envious* malicious   180 *purgers* purifiers, healers

For he can do no more than Caesar's arm
When Caesar's head is off.

CASSIUS   Yet I fear him;
184   For in the engrafted love he bears to Caesar –

BRUTUS
Alas, good Cassius, do not think of him.
If he love Caesar, all that he can do
187   Is to himself: take thought, and die for Caesar.
188   And that were much he should, for he is given
To sports, to wildness, and much company.

TREBONIUS
190   There is no fear in him. Let him not die;
For he will live, and laugh at this hereafter.
          Clock strikes.

BRUTUS
Peace, count the clock.

CASSIUS   The clock hath stricken three.

TREBONIUS
'Tis time to part.

CASSIUS   But it is doubtful yet
Whether Caesar will come forth today or no;
For he is superstitious grown of late,
196   Quite from the main opinion he held once
197   Of fantasy, of dreams and ceremonies.
198   It may be these apparent prodigies,
The unaccustomed terror of this night,
200   And the persuasion of his augurers,
May hold him from the Capitol today.

DECIUS
Never fear that. If he be so resolved
203   I can o'ersway him; for he loves to hear

---

184 *engrafted* deep-rooted   187 *take thought* succumb to melancholy   188
that . . . should it is unlikely that he would   190 *no fear* nothing to fear
196 *from the main* contrary to the strong   197 *fantasy* fancy (i.e., imagin-
ings); *ceremonies* portents   198 *apparent prodigies* manifest signs of disaster
200 *augurers* augurs (priests who interpreted omens)   203 *o'ersway* persuade

That unicorns may be betrayed with trees,   204
And bears with glasses, elephants with holes,   205
Lions with toils, and men with flatterers;   206
But when I tell him he hates flatterers,
He says he does, being then most flattered. Let me work,
For I can give his humor the true bent,   209
And I will bring him to the Capitol.   210

CASSIUS
Nay, we will all of us be there to fetch him.   211

BRUTUS
By the eighth hour. Is that the uttermost?   212

CINNA
Be that the uttermost, and fail not then.

METELLUS
Caius Ligarius doth bear Caesar hard,   214
Who rated him for speaking well of Pompey.   215
I wonder none of you have thought of him.

BRUTUS
Now good Metellus, go along by him.   217
He loves me well, and I have given him reasons.
Send him but hither, and I'll fashion him.   219

CASSIUS
The morning comes upon's. We'll leave you, Brutus.   220
And, friends, disperse yourselves; but all remember
What you have said, and show yourselves true Romans.

BRUTUS
Good gentlemen, look fresh and merrily.   223
Let not our looks put on our purposes;   224
But bear it as our Roman actors do,   225
With untired spirits and formal constancy.   226

---

204 *betrayed with trees* tricked into running their horns into tree trunks, thence easily captured 205 *glasses* mirrors (which were thought to bewilder bears); *holes* pits 206 *toils* snares 209 *humor* disposition; *bent* direction 211 *fetch* escort 212 *uttermost* latest 214 *hard* ill will 215 *rated* upbraided 217 *him* his house 219 *fashion* shape (to our purposes) 223 *fresh* brightly 224 *put on* display 225 *bear it* play your roles 226 *untired* alert; *formal constancy* proper self-possession

And so good morrow to you every one.
                              Exeunt all but Brutus.
Boy, Lucius! – Fast asleep? It is no matter.
229   Enjoy the honey-heavy dew of slumber.
230   Thou hast no figures nor no fantasies
      Which busy care draws in the brains of men;
      Therefore thou sleep'st so sound.
          Enter Portia.
PORTIA   Brutus, my lord.
BRUTUS
      Portia, what mean you? Wherefore rise you now?
234   It is not for your health thus to commit
      Your weak condition to the raw cold morning.
PORTIA
236   Nor for yours neither. You've ungently, Brutus,
      Stole from my bed; and yesternight at supper
      You suddenly arose, and walked about
239   Musing and sighing, with your arms across;
240   And when I asked you what the matter was,
      You stared upon me with ungentle looks.
      I urged you further, then you scratched your head,
      And too impatiently stamped with your foot.
      Yet I insisted; yet you answered not,
245   But with an angry wafture of your hand
      Gave sign for me to leave you. So I did,
      Fearing to strengthen that impatience
248   Which seemed too much enkindled, and withal
249   Hoping it was but an effect of humor,
250   Which sometime hath his hour with every man.
      It will not let you eat, nor talk, nor sleep;
      And could it work so much upon your shape
253   As it hath much prevailed on your condition,
254   I should not know you Brutus. Dear my lord,

---

229 *honey-heavy dew* i.e., sweetly drowsy refreshment   230 *figures* imagin-
ings   234 *for* good for; *commit* expose   236 *ungently* discourteously   239
across folded across your chest (a sign of melancholy)   245 *wafture* gesture
248 *withal* besides   249 *effect of humor* symptom of a temporary mood
250 *his* its   253 *condition* disposition   254 *know you* recognize you as

Make me acquainted with your cause of grief.
BRUTUS
I am not well in health, and that is all.
PORTIA
Brutus is wise, and were he not in health
He would embrace the means to come by it.   258
BRUTUS
Why, so I do. Good Portia, go to bed.
PORTIA
Is Brutus sick? And is it physical   260
To walk unbracèd and suck up the humors   261
Of the dank morning? What, is Brutus sick?
And will he steal out of his wholesome bed
To dare the vile contagion of the night,   264
And tempt the rheumy and unpurgèd air   265
To add unto his sickness? No, my Brutus,
You have some sick offense within your mind,   267
Which by the right and virtue of my place   268
I ought to know of. *(Kneeling)* And upon my knees,
I charm you by my once-commended beauty,   270
By all your vows of love, and that great vow
Which did incorporate and make us one,   272
That you unfold to me, your self, your half,   273
Why you are heavy, and what men tonight   274
Have had resort to you – for here have been
Some six or seven, who did hide their faces
Even from darkness.
BRUTUS   Kneel not, gentle Portia.
PORTIA   *Rising*
I should not need if you were gentle Brutus.
Within the bond of marriage, tell me, Brutus,

---

258 *embrace* adopt; *come by* regain   260 *physical* healthful   261 *unbracèd*
with open doublet; *suck up . . . humors* inhale . . . mists, dews   264 *vile . . .
night* (night air was thought to be poisonous)   265 *tempt* risk; *rheumy* moist;
unpurgèd not purified (by the sun)   267 *sick offense* harmful illness   268
virtue prerogative; *place* (as your wife)   270 *charm* solemnly entreat   272
incorporate make us one flesh   273 *unfold* disclose; *self* other self; *half* i.e.,
his wife   274 *heavy* sad

280 Is it excepted I should know no secrets
That appertain to you? Am I your self
282 But as it were in sort or limitation?
283 To keep with you at meals, comfort your bed,
284 And talk to you sometimes? Dwell I but in the suburbs
Of your good pleasure? If it be no more,
Portia is Brutus' harlot, not his wife.

BRUTUS
You are my true and honorable wife,
As dear to me as are the ruddy drops
289 That visit my sad heart.

PORTIA
290 If this were true, then should I know this secret.
291 I grant I am a woman, but withal
A woman that Lord Brutus took to wife.
I grant I am a woman, but withal
294 A woman well reputed, Cato's daughter.
Think you I am no stronger than my sex,
Being so fathered and so husbanded?
297 Tell me your counsels; I will not disclose 'em.
298 I have made strong proof of my constancy,
Giving myself a voluntary wound
300 Here in the thigh. Can I bear that with patience,
And not my husband's secrets?

BRUTUS   O ye gods,
Render me worthy of this noble wife!
    Knocking within.
Hark, hark, one knocks. Portia, go in a while,
And by and by thy bosom shall partake

---

280 *excepted* made an exception that   **282** *in . . . limitation* after a fashion; under restriction (a legalism)   **283** *keep* keep company   **284** *suburbs* outlying districts (notorious in London, and by analogy in ancient Rome, for their brothels and other disreputable haunts)   **289** *visit* afflict   **291** *withal* still   **294** *Cato* (Cato of Utica, famous for absolute moral integrity, fought with Pompey against Caesar and killed himself in 46 B.C. to avoid capture; he was Brutus's uncle as well as father-in-law)   **297** *counsels* secrets   **298** *proof* trial; *constancy* fortitude

The secrets of my heart.
All my engagements I will construe to thee,   306
All the charactery of my sad brows.   307
Leave me with haste.   *Exit Portia.*
                    Lucius, who's that knocks?
*Enter Lucius, and Ligarius, with a kerchief round his
head.*

LUCIUS
Here is a sick man that would speak with you.

BRUTUS
Caius Ligarius, that Metellus spake of.   310
    To Lucius
Boy, stand aside.   *Exit Lucius.*   311
                    Caius Ligarius, how?

LIGARIUS
Vouchsafe good morrow from a feeble tongue.   312

BRUTUS
O, what a time have you chose out, brave Caius,   313
To wear a kerchief! Would you were not sick!   314

LIGARIUS
I am not sick if Brutus have in hand
Any exploit worthy the name of honor.

BRUTUS
Such an exploit have I in hand, Ligarius,
Had you a healthful ear to hear of it.

LIGARIUS
By all the gods that Romans bow before,
I here discard my sickness.   320
    He pulls off his kerchief.
                    Soul of Rome,
Brave son derived from honorable loins,
Thou like an exorcist hast conjured up   322

---

306 *engagements* commitments; *construe* explain fully   307 *the charactery of*
that which is written in shorthand upon   311 *how* how are you   312
Vouchsafe deign to accept   313 *brave* noble   314 *To . . . kerchief* i.e., to be
sick   322 *exorcist* conjurer

323   My mortifièd spirit. Now bid me run,
      And I will strive with things impossible,
      Yea, get the better of them. What's to do?
BRUTUS
326   A piece of work that will make sick men whole.
LIGARIUS
327   But are not some whole that we must make sick?
BRUTUS
      That must we also. What it is, my Caius,
329   I shall unfold to thee as we are going
330   To whom it must be done.
LIGARIUS   Set on your foot,
      And with a heart new-fired I follow you
      To do I know not what; but it sufficeth
      That Brutus leads me on.
BRUTUS   Follow me then.   *Exeunt.*
                                *

∾ **II.2** *Thunder and lightning. Enter Julius Caesar
      in his nightgown.*

CAESAR
1   Nor heaven nor earth have been at peace tonight.
      Thrice hath Calpurnia in her sleep cried out
3   "Help, ho! They murder Caesar!" *(Calling)* Who's
      within?
         Enter a Servant.
SERVANT   My lord.
CAESAR
5   Go bid the priests do present sacrifice,
6   And bring me their opinions of success.

---

323 *mortifièd* deadened, as if dead   **326** *whole* healthy   **327** *make sick* i.e.,
kill   **329** *unfold* disclose   **330** *To whom* to the house of him to whom; *Set
on* advance
   II.2 Caesar's house   **s.d.** *nightgown* dressing gown   **1** *Nor . . . nor* neither . . . nor   **3** *Who's within* which of the servants is about   **5** *present* immediate   **6** *opinions of success* judgments of the success or failure of my plans

SERVANT I will, my lord.   *Exit.*
  Enter Calpurnia.
CALPURNIA
  What mean you, Caesar? Think you to walk forth?
  You shall not stir out of your house today.
CAESAR
  Caesar shall forth. The things that threatened me   10
  Ne'er looked but on my back; when they shall see
  The face of Caesar, they are vanishèd.
CALPURNIA
  Caesar, I never stood on ceremonies,   13
  Yet now they fright me. There is one within,
  Besides the things that we have heard and seen,
  Recounts most horrid sights seen by the watch.   16
  A lioness hath whelpèd in the streets,
  And graves have yawned and yielded up their dead.
  Fierce fiery warriors fight upon the clouds,
  In ranks and squadrons and right form of war,   20
  Which drizzled blood upon the Capitol.
  The noise of battle hurtled in the air.   22
  Horses do neigh, and dying men did groan,
  And ghosts did shriek and squeal about the streets.
  O Caesar, these things are beyond all use,   25
  And I do fear them.
CAESAR   What can be avoided
  Whose end is purposed by the mighty gods?
  Yet Caesar shall go forth, for these predictions
  Are to the world in general as to Caesar.   29
CALPURNIA
  When beggars die there are no comets seen;   30
  The heavens themselves blaze forth the death of princes.   31
CAESAR
  Cowards die many times before their deaths;

---

13 *stood on ceremonies* heeded portents   16 *watch* night watchmen   20 *right form* regular formation   22 *hurtled* clashed   25 *use* normal experience   29 *Are to* are as applicable to   31 *blaze forth* i.e., proclaim

The valiant never taste of death but once.
Of all the wonders that I yet have heard,
It seems to me most strange that men should fear,
Seeing that death, a necessary end,
Will come when it will come.
    Enter Servant.

                              What say the augurers?

SERVANT
They would not have you to stir forth today.
Plucking the entrails of an offering forth,
40   They could not find a heart within the beast.

CAESAR
41   The gods do this in shame of cowardice.
42   Caesar should be a beast without a heart
If he should stay at home today for fear.
No, Caesar shall not. Danger knows full well
That Caesar is more dangerous than he.
We are two lions littered in one day,
And I the elder and more terrible.
And Caesar shall go forth.

CALPURNIA   Alas, my lord,
49   Your wisdom is consumed in confidence.
50   Do not go forth today. Call it my fear
That keeps you in the house, and not your own.
We'll send Mark Antony to the Senate House,
And he shall say you are not well today.
Let me upon my knee prevail in this.
    She kneels.

CAESAR
Mark Antony shall say I am not well,
56   And for thy humor I will stay at home.
    Enter Decius.
Here's Decius Brutus; he shall tell them so.
    Calpurnia rises.

---

41 *in shame of cowardice* to put cowardice to shame   42 *should* would indeed
49 *consumed in confidence* destroyed by overconfidence   56 *humor* whim

DECIUS

    Caesar, all hail! Good morrow, worthy Caesar.

    I come to fetch you to the Senate House.   59

CAESAR

    And you are come in very happy time   60

    To bear my greeting to the senators

    And tell them that I will not come today.

    Cannot is false, and that I dare not, falser.

    I will not come today; tell them so, Decius.

CALPURNIA

    Say he is sick.

CAESAR   Shall Caesar send a lie?

    Have I in conquest stretched mine arm so far,

    To be afeard to tell graybeards the truth?

    Decius, go tell them Caesar will not come.

DECIUS

    Most mighty Caesar, let me know some cause,

    Lest I be laughed at when I tell them so.   70

CAESAR

    The cause is in my will; I will not come.

    That is enough to satisfy the Senate.

    But for your private satisfaction,

    Because I love you, I will let you know.

    Calpurnia here, my wife, stays me at home.   75

    She dreamt tonight she saw my statuë,   76

    Which like a fountain with an hundred spouts

    Did run pure blood; and many lusty Romans   78

    Came smiling and did bathe their hands in it.

    And these does she apply for warnings and portents   80

    Of evils imminent, and on her knee

    Hath begged that I will stay at home today.

DECIUS

    This dream is all amiss interpreted.

    It was a vision fair and fortunate.

---

59 *fetch* escort   60 *in . . . time* at a most opportune moment   75 *stays* keeps
76 *tonight* last night   78 *lusty* joyful   80 *apply for* interpret as

Your statue spouting blood in many pipes,
In which so many smiling Romans bathed,
Signifies that from you great Rome shall suck
Reviving blood, and that great men shall press
89   For tinctures, stains, relics, and cognizance.
90   This by Calpurnia's dream is signified.

CAESAR
And this way have you well expounded it.

DECIUS
I have, when you have heard what I can say.
93   And know it now: the Senate have concluded
To give this day a crown to mighty Caesar.
If you shall send them word you will not come,
96   Their minds may change. Besides, it were a mock
Apt to be rendered for someone to say
"Break up the Senate till another time,
When Caesar's wife shall meet with better dreams."
100   If Caesar hide himself, shall they not whisper
"Lo, Caesar is afraid"?
Pardon me, Caesar; for my dear dear love
103   To your proceeding bids me tell you this,
104   And reason to my love is liable.

CAESAR
How foolish do your fears seem now, Calpurnia!
I am ashamèd I did yield to them.
107   Give me my robe, for I will go.
    Enter Cassius, Brutus, Ligarius, Metellus, Casca,
    Trebonius, and Cinna.
And look where Cassius is come to fetch me.

CASSIUS
Good morrow, Caesar.

---

89 *tinctures* stains (with heraldic and alchemical associations); *relics* (as of holy martyrs); *cognizance* an identifying emblem worn by a nobleman's followers **93** *concluded* formally determined **96–97** *mock . . . rendered* sarcastic remark likely to be made **100** *shall* will indeed **103** *proceeding* advancement (?), career (?) **104** *reason . . . liable* i.e., my love outweighs my judgment in speaking thus freely to you **107** *robe* toga

CAESAR   Welcome, Cassius.
What, Brutus, are you stirred so early too?   *110*
Good morrow, Casca. Caius Ligarius,
Caesar was ne'er so much your enemy   *112*
As that same ague which hath made you lean.   *113*
What is't o'clock?
BRUTUS   Caesar, 'tis strucken eight.
CAESAR
I thank you for your pains and courtesy.
    Enter Antony.
See, Antony that revels long anights
Is notwithstanding up. Good morrow, Antony.
ANTONY
So to most noble Caesar.   *118*
CAESAR   *To Calpurnia*
                         Bid them prepare within.
I am to blame to be thus waited for.
                              Exit Calpurnia.
Now, Cinna. Now, Metellus. What, Trebonius!   *120*
I have an hour's talk in store for you.
Remember that you call on me today.
Be near me, that I may remember you.
TREBONIUS
Caesar, I will. *(Aside)* And so near will I be   *124*
That your best friends shall wish I had been further.
CAESAR
Good friends, go in and taste some wine with me,
And we, like friends, will straightway go together.
BRUTUS   *Aside*
That every like is not the same, O Caesar,   *128*
The heart of Brutus ernes to think upon.   *Exeunt.*   *129*
                         ✳

---

112 *enemy* (Ligarius, like Brutus, Cassius, and Cicero, had supported Pompey against Caesar)   113 *ague* fever   118 *So* likewise; *prepare* i.e., set out the wine   124–25 *And . . . further* (actually Trebonius lures Antony out of the way before the assassination)   128 *every . . . same* i.e., appearance is not always the same as reality   129 *ernes* grieves

ꝏ **II.3** *Enter Artemidorus, reading a letter.*

ARTEMIDORUS "Caesar, beware of Brutus. Take heed of
Cassius. Come not near Casca. Have an eye to Cinna.
Trust not Trebonius. Mark well Metellus Cimber. Decius Brutus loves thee not. Thou hast wronged Caius
Ligarius. There is but one mind in all these men, and it
6   is bent against Caesar. If thou beest not immortal, look
7   about you. Security gives way to conspiracy. The
mighty gods defend thee!
9   Thy lover,
10   Artemidorus."
Here will I stand till Caesar pass along,
12   And as a suitor will I give him this.
My heart laments that virtue cannot live
14   Out of the teeth of emulation.
If thou read this, O Caesar, thou mayst live.
16   If not, the fates with traitors do contrive.   *Exit.*

                                    *

ꝏ **II.4** *Enter Portia and Lucius.*

PORTIA
I prithee, boy, run to the Senate House.
Stay not to answer me, but get thee gone!
Why dost thou stay?
LUCIUS   To know my errand, madam.
PORTIA
I would have had thee there and here again
Ere I can tell thee what thou shouldst do there.
     Aside
6   O constancy, be strong upon my side;

II.3 A street near the Capitol   **6** *bent* directed   **7** *Security* overconfidence;
way path, opportunity   **9** *lover* friend, admirer   **12** *as a suitor* pretending to
be a petitioner   **14** *Out . . . emulation* i.e., beyond the reach of envious ri-
valry   **16** *contrive* conspire
     II.4 Brutus's house   **6** *constancy* self-control, fortitude

Set a huge mountain 'tween my heart and tongue.
I have a man's mind, but a woman's might.   8
How hard it is for women to keep counsel!   9
   To Lucius
Art thou here yet?   10

LUCIUS   Madam, what should I do?
Run to the Capitol, and nothing else?
And so return to you, and nothing else?

PORTIA
Yes, bring me word, boy, if thy lord look well,
For he went sickly forth; and take good note   14
What Caesar doth, what suitors press to him.
Hark, boy, what noise is that?

LUCIUS
I hear none, madam.

PORTIA
Prithee, listen well.
I heard a bustling rumor, like a fray,   19
And the wind brings it from the Capitol.   20

LUCIUS
Sooth, madam, I hear nothing.   21
   Enter the Soothsayer.

PORTIA
Come hither, fellow. Which way hast thou been?

SOOTHSAYER
At mine own house, good lady.

PORTIA
What is't o'clock?

SOOTHSAYER
About the ninth hour, lady.

PORTIA
Is Caesar yet gone to the Capitol?

---

8 *might* strength **9** *counsel* a secret (i.e., Brutus's secret, which he has told her according to his promise) **14** *take good note* observe well **19** *bustling . . . fray* confused noise such as in battle **21** *Sooth* truly

SOOTHSAYER
    Madam, not yet. I go to take my stand
    To see him pass on to the Capitol.
PORTIA
    Thou hast some suit to Caesar, hast thou not?
SOOTHSAYER
30   That I have, lady. If it will please Caesar
    To be so good to Caesar as to hear me,
    I shall beseech him to befriend himself.
PORTIA
    Why, know'st thou any harms intended towards him?
SOOTHSAYER
34   None that I know will be; much that I fear may chance.
    Good morrow to you.
      He moves away.
                  Here the street is narrow.
    The throng that follows Caesar at the heels,
37   Of senators, of praetors, common suitors,
    Will crowd a feeble man almost to death.
39   I'll get me to a place more void, and there
40   Speak to great Caesar as he comes along.   *Exit.*
PORTIA *Aside*
    I must go in. Ay me! How weak a thing
    The heart of woman is! O Brutus,
    The heavens speed thee in thine enterprise!
    Sure the boy heard me. *(To Lucius)* Brutus hath a suit
    That Caesar will not grant. *(Aside)* O, I grow faint!
      To Lucius
46   Run, Lucius, and commend me to my lord.
47   Say I am merry. Come to me again,
48   And bring me word what he doth say to thee.
                      Exeunt severally.

*

---

34 *chance* happen   37 *praetors* high-ranking judges in the administration of Roman law   39 *void* empty, spacious   46 *commend me* give my best love and wishes   47 *merry* in good spirits   48 **s.d.** *severally* separately

∾ **III.1** *Enter at one door Artemidorus, the Soothsayer,*
and Citizens. Flourish.
Enter at another door Caesar, Brutus, Cassius, Casca,
Decius, Metellus, Trebonius, Cinna, Ligarius, Antony,
Lepidus, Publius, Popillius, and other Senators.

CAESAR   *To the Soothsayer*
  The ides of March are come.
SOOTHSAYER
  Ay, Caesar, but not gone.
ARTEMIDORUS
  Hail, Caesar! Read this schedule.   3
DECIUS   *To Caesar*
  Trebonius doth desire you to o'erread
  At your best leisure this his humble suit.
ARTEMIDORUS
  O Caesar, read mine first, for mine's a suit
  That touches Caesar nearer. Read it, great Caesar.   7
CAESAR
  What touches us ourself shall be last served.   8
ARTEMIDORUS
  Delay not, Caesar, read it instantly.
CAESAR
  What, is the fellow mad?   10
PUBLIUS   *To Artemidorus*
                              Sirrah, give place.
CASSIUS   *To Artemidorus*
  What, urge you your petitions in the street?
  Come to the Capitol.   12
    They walk about the stage.
POPILLIUS   *Aside to Cassius*
  I wish your enterprise today may thrive.   13

III.1 At the Capitol 3 *schedule* document 7 *touches* concerns 8 *served* attended to 10 *Sirrah* (contemptuous form of address); *give place* get out of
the way 12 s.d. *They . . . stage* (representing a shift in location from the
street, outside, to the interior of the Capitol) 13 *enterprise* undertaking

CASSIUS
    What enterprise, Popillius?
POPILLIUS   Fare you well.
    He leaves Cassius, and makes to Caesar.
BRUTUS
    What said Popillius Laena?
CASSIUS
    He wished today our enterprise might thrive.
    I fear our purpose is discoverèd.
BRUTUS
18 Look how he makes to Caesar. Mark him.
CASSIUS
19 Casca, be sudden, for we fear prevention.
20 Brutus, what shall be done? If this be known,
21 Cassius or Caesar never shall turn back,
22 For I will slay myself.
BRUTUS   Cassius, be constant.
    Popillius Laena speaks not of our purposes,
24 For look, he smiles, and Caesar doth not change.
CASSIUS
    Trebonius knows his time, for look you, Brutus,
    He draws Mark Antony out of the way.
                         Exeunt Trebonius and Antony.
DECIUS
    Where is Metellus Cimber? Let him go
28 And presently prefer his suit to Caesar.
    Caesar sits.
BRUTUS
29 He is addressed. Press near, and second him.
CINNA
30 Casca, you are the first that rears your hand.
    *The Conspirators and the other Senators take their
    places.*

---

18 *makes to* advances toward   19 *sudden* quick; *prevention* being thwarted
21 *turn back* return alive   22 *constant* resolute   24 *Caesar . . . change* i.e.,
his expression does not change   28 *presently* immediately; *prefer* present   29
addressed ready

CAESAR
  Are we all ready? What is now amiss
  That Caesar and his Senate must redress?
METELLUS   *Coming forward and kneeling*
  Most high, most mighty, and most puissant Caesar,
  Metellus Cimber throws before thy seat
  An humble heart.   35
CAESAR   I must prevent thee, Cimber.
  These couchings and these lowly courtesies   36
  Might fire the blood of ordinary men,   37
  And turn preordinance and first decree   38
  Into the law of children. Be not fond   39
  To think that Caesar bears such rebel blood   40
  That will be thawed from the true quality   41
  With that which melteth fools: I mean sweet words,
  Low-crookèd curtsies, and base spaniel fawning.   43
  Thy brother by decree is banishèd.
  If thou dost bend and pray and fawn for him,
  I spurn thee like a cur out of my way.
  Know Caesar doth not wrong but with just cause,
  Nor without cause will he be satisfied.
METELLUS
  Is there no voice more worthy than my own
  To sound more sweetly in great Caesar's ear   *50*
  For the repealing of my banished brother?   *51*
BRUTUS   *Coming forward and kneeling*
  I kiss thy hand, but not in flattery, Caesar,
  Desiring thee that Publius Cimber may
  Have an immediate freedom of repeal.   54

---

35 *prevent* forestall 36 *couchings* stoopings; *courtesies* curtsies, bows 37 *blood* passions 38 *preordinance . . . decree* the original, time-honored laws by which men organized themselves into societies (i.e., the laws of man in accordance with the laws of nature and of God) 39 *the law . . . children* childish whims; *fond* so foolish as 40 *rebel* untrue to its own nature 41 *thawed* i.e., altered; *true* proper 43 *Low-crookèd* obsequious, dishonest; *spaniel* i.e., hypocritically flattering 51 *repealing* recalling from banishment 54 *freedom of repeal* permission to be recalled

CAESAR
What, Brutus?

CASSIUS   *Coming forward and kneeling*
           Pardon, Caesar; Caesar, pardon.
As low as to thy foot doth Cassius fall
57   To beg enfranchisement for Publius Cimber.

CAESAR
I could be well moved if I were as you.
59   If I could pray to move, prayers would move me.
60   But I am constant as the Northern Star,
61   Of whose true fixed and resting quality
62   There is no fellow in the firmament.
63   The skies are painted with unnumbered sparks;
      They are all fire, and every one doth shine;
65   But there's but one in all doth hold his place.
      So in the world: 'tis furnished well with men,
67   And men are flesh and blood, and apprehensive;
      Yet in the number I do know but one
69   That unassailable holds on his rank,
70   Unshaked of motion; and that I am he
      Let me a little show it even in this –
72   That I was constant Cimber should be banished,
      And constant do remain to keep him so.

CINNA   *Coming forward and kneeling*
74   O Caesar!

CAESAR   Hence! Wilt thou lift up Olympus?

DECIUS   *Coming forward with Ligarius and kneeling*
75   Great Caesar!

CAESAR   Doth not Brutus bootless kneel?

CASCA   *Coming forward and kneeling*

---

57 *enfranchisement* liberation   59 *pray to move* make pleas (myself)   60 *constant . . . Star* as fixed as the polestar (an ultimate symbol of constancy)   61 *resting* immovable   62 *fellow* equal   63 *painted* adorned   65 *hold* remain fixed in   67 *apprehensive* capable of knowing and reasoning   69 *holds . . . rank* remains fixed in his position   70 *Unshaked of motion* unmoved by persuasion   72 *constant* determined (resolutely)   74 *Olympus* a mountain in Greece, the home of the gods   75 *bootless* unavailingly

Speak hands for me.   76
> *They stab Caesar, Casca first, Brutus last.*

CAESAR   *Et tu, Brutè?* Then fall Caesar.
> *He dies.*

CINNA
Liberty! Freedom! Tyranny is dead!
Run hence, proclaim, cry it about the streets.

CASSIUS
Some to the common pulpits, and cry out   79
"Liberty, freedom, and enfranchisement!"   80

BRUTUS
People and senators, be not affrighted.
> *Exeunt in a tumult Lepidus, Popillius,*
> *other Senators, Artemidorus,*
> *Soothsayer, and Citizens.*

Fly not! Stand still! Ambition's debt is paid.   82

CASCA
Go to the pulpit, Brutus.

DECIUS
And Cassius too.

BRUTUS   Where's Publius?   85

CINNA
Here, quite confounded with this mutiny.   86

METELLUS
Stand fast together, lest some friend of Caesar's   87
Should chance –

BRUTUS
Talk not of standing. Publius, good cheer!   89
There is no harm intended to your person,   90
Nor to no Roman else – so tell them, Publius.

CASSIUS
And leave us, Publius, lest that the people,
Rushing on us, should do your age some mischief.   93

---

76 *Et tu, Brutè* you too (literally "and thou"), Brutus   79 *common pulpits*
public platforms for delivering speeches   82 *Ambition's debt* what was due to
Caesar's ambition   85 *Publius* an old senator   86 *quite confounded* too confused (to flee); *mutiny* tumult   87 *fast* close   89 *standing* organizing resis-
tance   93 *your age* i.e., you as an old man; *mischief* injury

BRUTUS
94   Do so; and let no man abide this deed
    But we the doers.   *Exit Publius.*
    Enter Trebonius.

CASSIUS
    Where is Antony?

TREBONIUS
97   Fled to his house, amazed.
    Men, wives, and children stare, cry out, and run,
99   As it were doomsday.

BRUTUS   Fates, we will know your pleasures.
100 That we shall die, we know; 'tis but the time
101 And drawing days out that men stand upon.

CASCA
    Why, he that cuts off twenty years of life
    Cuts off so many years of fearing death.

BRUTUS
    Grant that, and then is death a benefit.
    So are we Caesar's friends, that have abridged
    His time of fearing death. Stoop, Romans, stoop,
    And let us bathe our hands in Caesar's blood
    Up to the elbows, and besmear our swords;
109 Then walk we forth even to the marketplace,
110 And, waving our red weapons o'er our heads,
    Let's all cry "Peace, freedom, and liberty!"

CASSIUS
    Stoop, then, and wash.
    They smear their hands with Caesar's blood.
                  How many ages hence
    Shall this our lofty scene be acted over,
114 In states unborn and accents yet unknown!

BRUTUS
115 How many times shall Caesar bleed in sport,

---

94 *abide* stand the consequences of, be responsible for 97 *amazed* full of
consternation 99 *As* as if 100 *time* (specific time of death) 101 *draw-*
ing . . . upon prolonging life that men attach importance to 109 *the mar-*
ketplace the Roman Forum 114 *accents* languages 115 *in sport* for
entertainment (i.e., as plays)

That now on Pompey's basis lies along,　　116
No worthier than the dust!
CASSIUS　　　　　　　　　　So oft as that shall be,
So often shall the knot of us be called　　118
The men that gave their country liberty.
DECIUS
What, shall we forth?　　120
CASSIUS　　　　　　　　Ay, every man away.
Brutus shall lead, and we will grace his heels　　121
With the most boldest and best hearts of Rome.
　　Enter Antony's Servant.
BRUTUS
Soft; who comes here? A friend of Antony's.　　123
SERVANT　　*Kneeling and falling prostrate*
Thus, Brutus, did my master bid me kneel.
Thus did Mark Antony bid me fall down,
And, being prostrate, thus he bade me say:
"Brutus is noble, wise, valiant, and honest.　　127
Caesar was mighty, bold, royal, and loving.　　128
Say I love Brutus, and I honor him.
Say I feared Caesar, honored him, and loved him.　　*130*
If Brutus will vouchsafe that Antony
May safely come to him and be resolved　　132
How Caesar hath deserved to lie in death,
Mark Antony shall not love Caesar dead
So well as Brutus living, but will follow
The fortunes and affairs of noble Brutus
Thorough the hazards of this untrod state　　137
With all true faith." So says my master Antony.
BRUTUS
Thy master is a wise and valiant Roman.
I never thought him worse.　　*140*

---

116 *basis* pedestal of statue; *along* stretched out prostrate　118 *knot* group
(of conspirators)　120 *forth* go out into the city　121 *grace* do honor to
123 *Soft* hold on a moment　127 *honest* honorable　128 *royal* nobly munificent　132 *be resolved* have satisfactorily explained to him (?), be fully informed (?)　137 *Thorough* through; *this untrod state* these unprecedented
circumstances

141 Tell him, so please him come unto this place,
He shall be satisfied, and, by my honor,
143 Depart untouched.

SERVANT *Rising* I'll fetch him presently. *Exit.*

BRUTUS
144 I know that we shall have him well to friend.

CASSIUS
145 I wish we may. But yet have I a mind
146 That fears him much; and my misgiving still
147 Falls shrewdly to the purpose.

Enter Antony.

BRUTUS
But here comes Antony. Welcome, Mark Antony.

ANTONY
O mighty Caesar! Dost thou lie so low?
150 Are all thy conquests, glories, triumphs, spoils,
Shrunk to this little measure? Fare thee well.

To the Conspirators

I know not, gentlemen, what you intend –
153 Who else must be let blood, who else is rank.
If I myself, there is no hour so fit
As Caesar's death's hour, nor no instrument
Of half that worth as those your swords, made rich
With the most noble blood of all this world.
158 I do beseech ye, if you bear me hard,
159 Now, whilst your purpled hands do reek and smoke,
160 Fulfill your pleasure. Live a thousand years,
161 I shall not find myself so apt to die.
162 No place will please me so, no mean of death,
As here by Caesar, and by you cut off,

---

141 *so* if it should 143 *presently* at once 144 *to* as a 145 *mind* premoni-
tion 146 *fears* distrusts; *still* always 147 *Falls . . . purpose* turns out to be
very near the truth 153 *let blood* put to death (with a pun on "being bled
for medical purposes"); *rank* diseased (with a pun on "grown too strong")
158 *hard* a grudge 159 *purpled* i.e., with blood; *reek and smoke* i.e., steam
(with blood) 160 *Live* if I should live 161 *apt* ready 162 *so* so well; *mean*
manner, means

The choice and master spirits of this age.   164

BRUTUS
   O Antony, beg not your death of us!
   Though now we must appear bloody and cruel,
   As by our hands and this our present act
   You see we do, yet see you but our hands,
   And this the bleeding business they have done.
   Our hearts you see not; they are pitiful;   170
   And pity to the general wrong of Rome –
   As fire drives out fire, so pity pity –   172
   Hath done this deed on Caesar. For your part,   173
   To you our swords have leaden points, Mark Antony.   174
   Our arms, unstrung of malice, and our hearts   175
   Of brothers' temper, do receive you in   176
   With all kind love, good thoughts, and reverence.

CASSIUS
   Your voice shall be as strong as any man's   178
   In the disposing of new dignities.   179

BRUTUS
   Only be patient till we have appeased   180
   The multitude, beside themselves with fear,
   And then we will deliver you the cause   182
   Why I, that did love Caesar when I struck him,
   Have thus proceeded.

ANTONY   I doubt not of your wisdom.
   Let each man render me his bloody hand.
     He shakes hands with the Conspirators.
   First, Marcus Brutus, will I shake with you.
   Next, Caius Cassius, do I take your hand.
   Now, Decius Brutus, yours; now yours, Metellus;
   Yours, Cinna; and my valiant Casca, yours;

---

164 *choice* most select   **170** *pitiful* full of pity   **172** *pity pity* pity for the
general wrong drove out pity for Caesar   **173** *For your part* as for you   **174**
leaden blunt   **175** *unstrung of malice* given up their power to harm (the
image is of a bow with its string loosened)   **176** *temper* disposition   **178**
voice opinion, vote   **179** *dignities* offices of state   **180** *appeased* calmed
182 *deliver* report to

190   Though last, not least in love, yours, good Trebonius.
       Gentlemen all. Alas, what shall I say?
192   My credit now stands on such slippery ground
193   That one of two bad ways you must conceit me:
       Either a coward or a flatterer.
       That I did love thee, Caesar, O, 'tis true.
       If then thy spirit look upon us now,
197   Shall it not grieve thee dearer than thy death
       To see thy Antony making his peace,
       Shaking the bloody fingers of thy foes –
200   Most noble! – in the presence of thy corpse?
       Had I as many eyes as thou hast wounds,
       Weeping as fast as they stream forth thy blood,
203   It would become me better than to close
       In terms of friendship with thine enemies.
205   Pardon me, Julius. Here wast thou bayed, brave hart;
       Here didst thou fall, and here thy hunters stand
207   Signed in thy spoil and crimsoned in thy lethë.
       O world, thou wast the forest to this hart;
       And this indeed, O world, the heart of thee.
210   How like a deer strucken by many princes
       Dost thou here lie!

CASSIUS
       Mark Antony.

ANTONY
       Pardon me, Caius Cassius.
       The enemies of Caesar shall say this;
215   Then in a friend it is cold modesty.

CASSIUS
       I blame you not for praising Caesar so;

---

192 *My credit* my reputation as Caesar's friend (?), trust in me (?)   193 *conceit* judge   197 *dearer* more keenly   203 *close* conclude an agreement   205 *bayed* brought to bay; *hart* stag (with a pun on *heart,* which Antony continues to develop)   207 *Signed . . . spoil* marked with the signs of your slaughter; *lethë* (Lethe was the river of forgetfulness in Hades, but came to mean more generally "oblivion"; here, the allusion seems to be to Caesar's lifeblood)   210 *strucken* struck down   215 *modesty* moderation

But what compact mean you to have with us?   217
Will you be pricked in number of our friends,   218
Or shall we on, and not depend on you?   219
ANTONY
Therefore I took your hands, but was indeed   220
Swayed from the point by looking down on Caesar.
Friends am I with you all, and love you all
Upon this hope: that you shall give me reasons
Why and wherein Caesar was dangerous.
BRUTUS
Or else were this a savage spectacle.
Our reasons are so full of good regard,   226
That were you, Antony, the son of Caesar,
You should be satisfied.
ANTONY   That's all I seek;
And am, moreover, suitor that I may   229
Produce his body to the marketplace,   230
And in the pulpit, as becomes a friend,   231
Speak in the order of his funeral.   232
BRUTUS
You shall, Mark Antony.
CASSIUS   Brutus, a word with you.
    Aside to Brutus
You know not what you do. Do not consent
That Antony speak in his funeral.
Know you how much the people may be moved
By that which he will utter?   237
BRUTUS   *Aside to Cassius*
                          By your pardon,
I will myself into the pulpit first,
And show the reason of our Caesar's death.
What Antony shall speak I will protest   240
He speaks by leave and by permission;

---

217 *compact* agreement   218 *pricked in number of* be counted among   219
on proceed   226 *good regard* sound considerations   229 *suitor* petitioner
230 *Produce* bring forth   231 *pulpit* rostrum   232 *order* ceremony   237 *By
your pardon* with your permission   240 *protest* proclaim

And that we are contented Caesar shall
243   Have all true rites and lawful ceremonies,
244   It shall advantage more than do us wrong.

CASSIUS   *Aside to Brutus*
245   I know not what may fall. I like it not.

BRUTUS
Mark Antony, here, take you Caesar's body.
You shall not in your funeral speech blame us;
But speak all good you can devise of Caesar,
And say you do't by our permission;
250   Else shall you not have any hand at all
251   About his funeral. And you shall speak
In the same pulpit whereto I am going,
After my speech is ended.

ANTONY
Be it so;
I do desire no more.

BRUTUS
Prepare the body then, and follow us.

Exeunt all but Antony.

ANTONY
O pardon me, thou bleeding piece of earth,
That I am meek and gentle with these butchers.
Thou art the ruins of the noblest man
260   That ever livèd in the tide of times.
261   Woe to the hand that shed this costly blood!
Over thy wounds now do I prophesy –
Which like dumb mouths do ope their ruby lips
To beg the voice and utterance of my tongue –
A curse shall light upon the limbs of men;
Domestic fury and fierce civil strife
267   Shall cumber all the parts of Italy;
268   Blood and destruction shall be so in use,
And dreadful objects so familiar,

---

243 *true* proper   244 *advantage* benefit (us)   245 *fall* happen   251 *About* in   260 *tide of times* course of history   261 *costly* precious   267 *cumber* burden   268 *in use* common

That mothers shall but smile when they behold   *270*
Their infants quartered with the hands of war,   271
All pity choked with custom of fell deeds;   272
And Caesar's spirit, ranging for revenge,   273
With Atë by his side come hot from hell,   274
Shall in these confines with a monarch's voice   275
Cry "havoc!" and let slip the dogs of war,   276
That this foul deed shall smell above the earth   277
With carrion men, groaning for burial.   278
    Enter Octavius' Servant.
You serve Octavius Caesar, do you not?

SERVANT
I do, Mark Antony.   *280*

ANTONY
Caesar did write for him to come to Rome.

SERVANT
He did receive his letters, and is coming,
And bid me say to you by word of mouth –
    Seeing the body
O Caesar!

ANTONY
Thy heart is big. Get thee apart and weep.   285
Passion, I see, is catching, for mine eyes,   286
Seeing those beads of sorrow stand in thine,
Began to water. Is thy master coming?

SERVANT
He lies tonight within seven leagues of Rome.   289

ANTONY
Post back with speed and tell him what hath chanced.   290
Here is a mourning Rome, a dangerous Rome,
No Rome of safety for Octavius yet.
Hie hence and tell him so. Yet stay awhile.   293

---

271 *quartered* cut in pieces   272 *custom of fell* familiarity with cruel   273 *ranging* roving (in search of prey)   274 *Atë* Greek goddess of discord   275 *confines* regions   276 *havoc* (the signal for unlimited slaughter); *let slip* unleash   277 *That* so that   278 *carrion* dead and rotting   285 *big* swollen with grief   286 *Passion* sorrow   289 *lies* stays; *seven leagues* twenty miles   290 *Post* ride quickly   293 *Hie* hasten

Thou shalt not back till I have borne this corpse
295 Into the marketplace. There shall I try
In my oration how the people take
297 The cruel issue of these bloody men;
298 According to the which thou shalt discourse
To young Octavius of the state of things.
300 Lend me your hand.   *Exeunt with Caesar's body.*

*

∾ **III.2** *Enter Brutus and Cassius, with the Plebeians.*

ALL THE PLEBEIANS
1   We will be satisfied! Let us be satisfied!
BRUTUS
2   Then follow me, and give me audience, friends.
        Aside to Cassius
     Cassius, go you into the other street,
4   And part the numbers.
        To the Plebeians
     Those that will hear me speak, let 'em stay here;
     Those that will follow Cassius, go with him;
7   And public reasons shall be renderèd
     Of Caesar's death.
        Brutus ascends to the pulpit.
FIRST PLEBEIAN   I will hear Brutus speak.
SECOND PLEBEIAN
     I will hear Cassius, and compare their reasons
10   When severally we hear them renderèd.
                    Exit Cassius, with some Plebeians.
        Enter Brutus on the upper stage, as if in the pulpit.
THIRD PLEBEIAN
     The noble Brutus is ascended. Silence.

---

295 *try* test   **297** *cruel issue* result of the cruelty   **298** *the which* the result of my test

III.2 The Forum   **1** *be satisfied* given a full explanation   **2** *audience* a hearing   **4** *part the numbers* divide the crowd   **7** *public reasons* (1) reasons having to do with the general good (?), (2) reasons in explanation to the public (?)   **10** *severally* separately

BRUTUS

Be patient till the last. 12

Romans, countrymen, and lovers, hear me for my 13
cause, and be silent that you may hear. Believe me for 14
mine honor, and have respect to mine honor, that you 15
may believe. Censure me in your wisdom, and awake 16
your senses, that you may the better judge. If there be 17
any in this assembly, any dear friend of Caesar's, to him
I say that Brutus' love to Caesar was no less than his. If
then that friend demand why Brutus rose against Cae- 20
sar, this is my answer: not that I loved Caesar less, but
that I loved Rome more. Had you rather Caesar were
living, and die all slaves, than that Caesar were dead, to
live all free men? As Caesar loved me, I weep for him.
As he was fortunate, I rejoice at it. As he was valiant, I
honor him. But as he was ambitious, I slew him. There
is tears for his love, joy for his fortune, honor for his
valor, and death for his ambition. Who is here so base
that would be a bondman? If any, speak, for him have I 29
offended. Who is here so rude that would not be a 30
Roman? If any, speak, for him have I offended. Who is
here so vile that will not love his country? If any, speak,
for him have I offended. I pause for a reply.

ALL THE PLEBEIANS   None, Brutus, none.

BRUTUS   Then none have I offended. I have done no
more to Caesar than you shall do to Brutus. The ques- 36
tion of his death is enrolled in the Capitol, his glory not 37
extenuated wherein he was worthy, nor his offenses en- 38
forced for which he suffered death.

*Enter Mark Antony, with others bearing Caesar's body
in a coffin.*

---

12 *last* end of my speech   13 *lovers* dear friends   13–14 *my cause* i.e., the
cause of freedom   14 *for* on account of   15 *have . . . honor* remember that I
am honorable   16 *Censure* judge   17 *senses* reason   29 *bondman* slave   30
offended wronged; *rude* barbarous   36 *shall do* i.e., if Brutus should so offend
36–37 *question of* reasons for   37 *enrolled in* recorded in the archives of   38
extenuated understated   38–39 *enforced* overstated

40 Here comes his body, mourned by Mark Antony, who,
though he had no hand in his death, shall receive the
42 benefit of his dying: a place in the commonwealth – as
which of you shall not? With this I depart: that as I
44 slew my best lover for the good of Rome, I have the
same dagger for myself when it shall please my country
to need my death.

ALL THE PLEBEIANS   Live, Brutus, live, live!

FIRST PLEBEIAN
Bring him with triumph home unto his house.

FOURTH PLEBEIAN
Give him a statue with his ancestors.

THIRD PLEBEIAN
50 Let him be Caesar.

FIFTH PLEBEIAN   Caesar's better parts
Shall be crowned in Brutus.

FIRST PLEBEIAN
We'll bring him to his house with shouts and clamors.

BRUTUS
My countrymen.

FOURTH PLEBEIAN   Peace, silence. Brutus speaks.

FIRST PLEBEIAN
Peace, ho!

BRUTUS
Good countrymen, let me depart alone,
And, for my sake, stay here with Antony.
57 Do grace to Caesar's corpse, and grace his speech
58 Tending to Caesar's glories, which Mark Antony,
By our permission, is allowed to make.
60 I do entreat you, not a man depart
Save I alone till Antony have spoke.   *Exit.*

FIRST PLEBEIAN
Stay, ho, and let us hear Mark Antony.

---

42 *place* i.e., as a free Roman   44 *lover* friend   50 *parts* qualities   57 *Do . . .
speech* pay respect to Caesar's corpse and courteously hear Antony's speech
58 *Tending* relating

THIRD PLEBEIAN
Let him go up into the public chair.   63
We'll hear him. Noble Antony, go up.

ANTONY
For Brutus' sake I am beholden to you.   65
Antony ascends to the pulpit.

FIFTH PLEBEIAN
What does he say of Brutus?

THIRD PLEBEIAN   He says, for Brutus' sake
He finds himself beholden to us all.

FIFTH PLEBEIAN
'Twere best he speak no harm of Brutus here!

FIRST PLEBEIAN
This Caesar was a tyrant.

THIRD PLEBEIAN   Nay, that's certain.
We are blessed that Rome is rid of him.   70
Enter Antony in the pulpit.

FOURTH PLEBEIAN
Peace, let us hear what Antony can say.

ANTONY
You gentle Romans.

ALL THE PLEBEIANS   Peace, ho! Let us hear him.

ANTONY
Friends, Romans, countrymen, lend me your ears.
I come to bury Caesar, not to praise him.
The evil that men do lives after them;
The good is oft interrèd with their bones.
So let it be with Caesar. The noble Brutus
Hath told you Caesar was ambitious.
If it were so, it was a grievous fault,
And grievously hath Caesar answered it.   80
Here, under leave of Brutus and the rest –   81
For Brutus is an honorable man,
So are they all, all honorable men –
Come I to speak in Caesar's funeral.

---

63 *chair* pulpit, rostrum   65 *beholden* obliged   80 *answered it* paid the
penalty   81 *under leave* by permission

85 He was my friend, faithful and just to me.
But Brutus says he was ambitious,
And Brutus is an honorable man.
He hath brought many captives home to Rome,
89 Whose ransoms did the general coffers fill.
90 Did this in Caesar seem ambitious?
When that the poor have cried, Caesar hath wept.
Ambition should be made of sterner stuff.
Yet Brutus says he was ambitious,
And Brutus is an honorable man.
You all did see that on the Lupercal
I thrice presented him a kingly crown,
Which he did thrice refuse. Was this ambition?
Yet Brutus says he was ambitious,
And sure he is an honorable man.
100 I speak not to disprove what Brutus spoke,
But here I am to speak what I do know.
You all did love him once, not without cause.
What cause withholds you then to mourn for him?
O judgment, thou art fled to brutish beasts,
And men have lost their reason!
     He weeps.
                              Bear with me.
My heart is in the coffin there with Caesar,
And I must pause till it come back to me.

FIRST PLEBEIAN
Methinks there is much reason in his sayings.

FOURTH PLEBEIAN
If thou consider rightly of the matter,
110 Caesar has had great wrong.

THIRD PLEBEIAN   Has he not, masters?
I fear there will a worse come in his place.

FIFTH PLEBEIAN
Marked ye his words? He would not take the crown,
Therefore 'tis certain he was not ambitious.

---

85 *just* entirely reliable   89 *general coffers* public treasury

FIRST PLEBEIAN
 If it be found so, some will dear abide it.   114
FOURTH PLEBEIAN
 Poor soul, his eyes are red as fire with weeping.
THIRD PLEBEIAN
 There's not a nobler man in Rome than Antony.
FIFTH PLEBEIAN
 Now mark him; he begins again to speak.
ANTONY
 But yesterday the word of Caesar might   118
 Have stood against the world. Now lies he there,
 And none so poor to do him reverence.   120
 O masters, if I were disposed to stir
 Your hearts and minds to mutiny and rage,   122
 I should do Brutus wrong, and Cassius wrong,
 Who, you all know, are honorable men.
 I will not do them wrong. I rather choose
 To wrong the dead, to wrong myself and you,
 Than I will wrong such honorable men.
 But here's a parchment with the seal of Caesar.
 I found it in his closet. 'Tis his will.   129
 Let but the commons hear this testament –   130
 Which, pardon me, I do not mean to read –
 And they would go and kiss dead Caesar's wounds,
 And dip their napkins in his sacred blood,   133
 Yea, beg a hair of him for memory,
 And, dying, mention it within their wills,
 Bequeathing it as a rich legacy
 Unto their issue.   137
FIFTH PLEBEIAN
 We'll hear the will. Read it, Mark Antony.
ALL THE PLEBEIANS
 The will, the will! We will hear Caesar's will.

———————
114 *dear abide* pay a heavy penalty for   118 *But* only   120 *so poor* base
enough   122 *mutiny* riot   129 *closet* study (?), cabinet for private papers (?)
130 *commons* plebeians   133 *napkins* handkerchiefs (the implication is that
Caesar is a martyr whose relics – *blood, hair* – should be regarded as holy)
137 *issue* children

ANTONY

140   Have patience, gentle friends, I must not read it.
141   It is not meet you know how Caesar loved you.
       You are not wood, you are not stones, but men;
       And, being men, hearing the will of Caesar,
       It will inflame you, it will make you mad.
       'Tis good you know not that you are his heirs,
       For if you should, O what would come of it?

FIFTH PLEBEIAN

       Read the will. We'll hear it, Antony.
       You shall read us the will, Caesar's will.

ANTONY

149   Will you be patient? Will you stay a while?
150   I have o'ershot myself to tell you of it.
       I fear I wrong the honorable men
       Whose daggers have stabbed Caesar; I do fear it.

FIFTH PLEBEIAN   They were traitors. Honorable men?

ALL THE PLEBEIANS   The will, the testament!

FOURTH PLEBEIAN   They were villains, murderers. The
    will, read the will!

ANTONY

       You will compel me then to read the will?
       Then make a ring about the corpse of Caesar,
       And let me show you him that made the will.
160   Shall I descend? And will you give me leave?

ALL THE PLEBEIANS
       Come down.

FOURTH PLEBEIAN   Descend.

THIRD PLEBEIAN   You shall have leave.
       Antony descends from the pulpit.

FIFTH PLEBEIAN   A ring.
162   Stand round.

FIRST PLEBEIAN   Stand from the hearse. Stand from the
    body.

---

141 *meet* fitting that   149 *stay* wait   150 *o'ershot myself* gone further than I
intended   162 *hearse* bier

FOURTH PLEBEIAN
    Room for Antony, most noble Antony!
    Enter Antony below, on the main stage.
ANTONY
    Nay, press not so upon me. Stand farre off.   164
ALL THE PLEBEIANS
    Stand back! Room! Bear back!   165
ANTONY
    If you have tears, prepare to shed them now.
    You all do know this mantle. I remember   167
    The first time ever Caesar put it on.
    'Twas on a summer's evening in his tent,
    That day he overcame the Nervii.   170
    Look, in this place ran Cassius' dagger through.
    See what a rent the envious Casca made.   172
    Through this the well-belovèd Brutus stabbed;
    And as he plucked his cursèd steel away,
    Mark how the blood of Caesar followed it,
    As rushing out of doors to be resolved   176
    If Brutus so unkindly knocked or no –   177
    For Brutus, as you know, was Caesar's angel.   178
    Judge, O you gods, how dearly Caesar loved him!
    This was the most unkindest cut of all.   180
    For when the noble Caesar saw him stab,
    Ingratitude, more strong than traitors' arms,
    Quite vanquished him. Then burst his mighty heart,
    And in his mantle muffling up his face,
    Even at the base of Pompey's statue,   185
    Which all the while ran blood, great Caesar fell.
    O, what a fall was there, my countrymen!
    Then I, and you, and all of us fell down,

---

164 *farre* farther (an obsolete comparative of "far")   165 *Bear* move   167
mantle cloak (here, a toga)   170 *Nervii* a tribe defeated by Caesar in 57 B.C.
in one of the most decisive victories in the Gallic Wars   172 *envious* malicious   176 *As* as if; *be resolved* learn for certain   177 *unkindly* unnaturally
and cruelly   178 *angel* "darling" (i.e., favorite who could do no wrong)
180 *most unkindest* cruelest and most unnatural   185 *base* pedestal

189   Whilst bloody treason flourished over us.

190   O now you weep, and I perceive you feel

191   The dint of pity. These are gracious drops.

    Kind souls – what – weep you when you but behold

193   Our Caesar's vesture wounded? Look you here.

194   Here is himself, marred, as you see, with traitors.

      He uncovers Caesar's body.

FIRST PLEBEIAN

  O piteous spectacle!

FOURTH PLEBEIAN   O noble Caesar!

THIRD PLEBEIAN

  O woeful day!

FIFTH PLEBEIAN

  O traitors, villains!

FIRST PLEBEIAN   O most bloody sight!

FOURTH PLEBEIAN   We will be revenged.

ALL THE PLEBEIANS

199   Revenge! About! Seek! Burn! Fire! Kill! Slay!

200   Let not a traitor live!

ANTONY   Stay, countrymen.

FIRST PLEBEIAN   Peace there, hear the noble Antony.

FOURTH PLEBEIAN   We'll hear him, we'll follow him, we'll

  die with him!

ANTONY

  Good friends, sweet friends, let me not stir you up

  To such a sudden flood of mutiny.

  They that have done this deed are honorable.

207   What private griefs they have, alas, I know not,

  That made them do it. They are wise and honorable,

  And will no doubt with reasons answer you.

210   I come not, friends, to steal away your hearts.

  I am no orator as Brutus is,

  But, as you know me all, a plain blunt man

  That love my friend; and that they know full well

---

189 *flourished* swaggered and brandished its sword in triumph   191 *dint* impression; *gracious* full of grace, becoming   193 *vesture* garment   194 *marred* mangled; *with* by   199 *About* to work   200 *Stay* wait   207 *private griefs* personal grievances

That gave me public leave to speak of him.   214
For I have neither wit, nor words, nor worth,   215
Action, nor utterance, nor the power of speech,   216
To stir men's blood. I only speak right on.   217
I tell you that which you yourselves do know,
Show you sweet Caesar's wounds, poor poor dumb
   mouths,
And bid them speak for me. But were I Brutus,   220
And Brutus Antony, there were an Antony
Would ruffle up your spirits, and put a tongue   222
In every wound of Caesar that should move
The stones of Rome to rise and mutiny.   224

ALL THE PLEBEIANS
   We'll mutiny.
FIRST PLEBEIAN   We'll burn the house of Brutus.
THIRD PLEBEIAN
   Away then! Come, seek the conspirators.
ANTONY
   Yet hear me, countrymen, yet hear me speak.
ALL THE PLEBEIANS
   Peace, ho! Hear Antony, most noble Antony.
ANTONY
   Why, friends, you go to do you know not what.
   Wherein hath Caesar thus deserved your loves?   230
   Alas, you know not. I must tell you then.
   You have forgot the will I told you of.
ALL THE PLEBEIANS
   Most true. The will. Let's stay and hear the will.
ANTONY
   Here is the will, and under Caesar's seal.
   To every Roman citizen he gives –
   To every several man – seventy-five drachmas.   236

---

214 *public . . . speak* permission to speak in public   215 *wit* intelligence;
worth stature   216 *Action* skillful use of gesture; *utterance* good delivery
217 *right on* straightforwardly, just as I think it   222 *ruffle* stir   224 *mutiny*
riot   236 *several* individual; *drachmas* Greek silver coins

FOURTH PLEBEIAN
Most noble Caesar! We'll revenge his death.
THIRD PLEBEIAN
238 O royal Caesar!
ANTONY   Hear me with patience.
ALL THE PLEBEIANS   Peace, ho!
ANTONY
Moreover he hath left you all his walks,
240 His private arbors, and new-planted orchards,
On this side Tiber. He hath left them you,
242 And to your heirs for ever – common pleasures
To walk abroad and recreate yourselves.
Here was a Caesar. When comes such another?
FIRST PLEBEIAN
Never, never! Come, away, away!
246 We'll burn his body in the holy place,
And with the brands fire the traitors' houses.
Take up the body.
FOURTH PLEBEIAN   Go, fetch fire!
250 THIRD PLEBEIAN   Pluck down benches!
251 FIFTH PLEBEIAN   Pluck down forms, windows, anything!
            Exeunt Plebeians with Caesar's body.

ANTONY
252 Now let it work. Mischief, thou art afoot.
253 Take thou what course thou wilt.
     Enter Octavius' Servant.
                   How now, fellow?
SERVANT
Sir, Octavius is already come to Rome.
ANTONY
Where is he?
SERVANT
He and Lepidus are at Caesar's house.

---

238 *royal* nobly munificent; *Peace* silence   **240** *orchards* gardens   **242** *common pleasures* public parks   **246** *holy place* (where the most sacred temples were in Rome)   **250** *Pluck down* wrench loose, tear out   **251** *forms* long benches; *windows* shutters   **252** *work* have its full effect   **253** *fellow* (form of address to social inferiors)

ANTONY
    And thither will I straight to visit him.   257
    He comes upon a wish. Fortune is merry,   258
    And in this mood will give us anything.

SERVANT
    I heard him say Brutus and Cassius   260
    Are rid like madmen through the gates of Rome.   261

ANTONY
    Belike they had some notice of the people,   262
    How I had moved them. Bring me to Octavius.   263

                              Exeunt.

✻

❧ **III.3** *Enter Cinna the poet.*

CINNA
    I dreamt tonight that I did feast with Caesar,   1
    And things unlucky charge my fantasy.   2
    I have no will to wander forth of doors,   3
    Yet something leads me forth.
      Enter the Plebeians.

FIRST PLEBEIAN   What is your name?
SECOND PLEBEIAN   Whither are you going?
THIRD PLEBEIAN   Where do you dwell?
FOURTH PLEBEIAN   Are you a married man or a bachelor?
SECOND PLEBEIAN   Answer every man directly.   9
FIRST PLEBEIAN   Ay, and briefly.   10
FOURTH PLEBEIAN   Ay, and wisely.
THIRD PLEBEIAN   Ay, and truly, you were best.   12
CINNA   What is my name? Whither am I going? Where
    do I dwell? Am I a married man or a bachelor? Then to

---

257 *straight* at once   258 *upon a wish* exactly as I might have wished; *merry*
in a good mood (toward us)   261 *Are rid* have ridden   262 *Belike* probably;
notice of news about   263 *Bring* escort
    III.3 A street in Rome   1 *tonight* last night   2 *things . . . fantasy* bad
omens oppress my thoughts   3 *forth* out   9 *directly* plainly   12 *you were
best* you'd better

answer every man directly and briefly, wisely and truly: wisely, I say, I am a bachelor.

17 SECOND PLEBEIAN   That's as much as to say they are fools
18   that marry. You'll bear me a bang for that, I fear. Proceed directly.

20 CINNA   Directly I am going to Caesar's funeral.

FIRST PLEBEIAN   As a friend or an enemy?

CINNA   As a friend.

SECOND PLEBEIAN   That matter is answered directly.

FOURTH PLEBEIAN   For your dwelling – briefly.

CINNA   Briefly, I dwell by the Capitol.

THIRD PLEBEIAN   Your name, sir, truly.

CINNA   Truly, my name is Cinna –

FIRST PLEBEIAN   Tear him to pieces! He's a conspirator.

CINNA   I am Cinna the *poet!* I am Cinna the *poet!*

30 FOURTH PLEBEIAN   Tear him for his bad verses, tear him for his bad verses.

CINNA   I am not Cinna the conspirator!

FOURTH PLEBEIAN   It is no matter, his name's Cinna.
34   Pluck but his name out of his heart, and turn him going.

THIRD PLEBEIAN   Tear him, tear him!

> *They set upon Cinna.*

Come, brands, ho! Firebrands! To Brutus', to Cassius'! Burn all! Some to Decius' house, and some to Casca's; some to Ligarius'. Away, go!

> *Exeunt all the Plebeians, with Cinna.*

*

❧ **IV.1**   *Enter Antony with papers, Octavius, and Lepidus.*

ANTONY
1   These many, then, shall die; their names are pricked.

17–18 *they . . . marry* (proverbial)   18 *bear me a bang* get a blow from me
34 *Pluck* tear   34–35 *turn him going* send him packing
IV.1 Antony's house in Rome   1 *pricked* marked down (on a list)

OCTAVIUS *To Lepidus*
  Your brother too must die. Consent you, Lepidus?
LEPIDUS
  I do consent.
OCTAVIUS Prick him down, Antony.
LEPIDUS
  Upon condition Publius shall not live, 4
  Who is your sister's son, Mark Antony.
ANTONY
  He shall not live. Look, with a spot I damn him. 6
  But Lepidus, go you to Caesar's house;
  Fetch the will hither, and we shall determine
  How to cut off some charge in legacies. 9
LEPIDUS What, shall I find you here? 10
OCTAVIUS Or here or at the Capitol. *Exit Lepidus.* 11
ANTONY
  This is a slight, unmeritable man, 12
  Meet to be sent on errands. Is it fit, 13
  The threefold world divided, he should stand 14
  One of the three to share it?
OCTAVIUS So you thought him,
  And took his voice who should be pricked to die 16
  In our black sentence and proscription. 17
ANTONY
  Octavius, I have seen more days than you, 18
  And though we lay these honors on this man
  To ease ourselves of divers sland'rous loads, 20
  He shall but bear them as the ass bears gold,
  To groan and sweat under the business, 22
  Either led or driven as we point the way;

---

4 *Upon condition* provided that 6 *spot* mark; *damn* condemn 9 *cut . . . charge* reduce the outlay of the estate (by altering the will) 11 *Or* either 12 *slight, unmeritable* insignificant and unworthy 13 *Meet* fit 14 *The . . . divided* the world being divided among the three triumvirs into three parts (Europe, Africa, and Asia) 16 *voice* vote 17 *black* i.e., death; *proscription* condemnation to death or exile 18 *have . . . days* am older (i.e., more experienced) 20 *ease . . . loads* lighten for ourselves some of the charges that will be brought against us 22 *business* work done by beasts

And having brought our treasure where we will,
25 Then take we down his load, and turn him off,
26 Like to the empty ass, to shake his ears
27 And graze in commons.
OCTAVIUS   You may do your will;
    But he's a tried and valiant soldier.
ANTONY
    So is my horse, Octavius, and for that
30 I do appoint him store of provender.
    It is a creature that I teach to fight,
32 To wind, to stop, to run directly on,
33 His corporal motion governed by my spirit;
34 And in some taste is Lepidus but so.
    He must be taught, and trained, and bid go forth –
36 A barren-spirited fellow, one that feeds
    On objects, arts, and imitations,
38 Which, out of use and staled by other men,
39 Begin his fashion. Do not talk of him
40 But as a property. And now, Octavius,
41 Listen great things. Brutus and Cassius
42 Are levying powers. We must straight make head.
43 Therefore let our alliance be combined,
44 Our best friends made, our meinies stretched,
    And let us presently go sit in council,
46 How covert matters may be best disclosed,
47 And open perils surest answerèd.

---

25 *turn him off* send him packing 26 *empty* unburdened 27 *commons*
public pasture 30 *appoint* provide; *store* a supply 32 *To wind ... on* to
turn, to stop suddenly, to resume running immediately 33 *corporal* bodily
34 *taste* degree; *so* the same 36 *barren-spirited* without initiative, unoriginal
36–37 *feeds . . . imitations* nourishes his spirit with curiosities, artificial con-
trivances, and following of fashions 38 *staled* cheapened, worn out 39
Begin his fashion he then adopts as fashionable 40 *property* chattel (?), tool
(?) 41 *Listen* hear 42 *powers* armies; *straight make head* immediately raise
an army 43 *combined* strengthened 44 *made* mustered; *meinies* bands of
followers; *stretched* (1) augmented, (2) used to their fullest advantage 46
How . . . disclosed to determine how hidden dangers may best be discovered
47 *surest answerèd* most safely met

OCTAVIUS
Let us do so, for we are at the stake   48
And bayed about with many enemies;
And some that smile have in their hearts, I fear,   50
Millions of mischiefs.   *Exeunt.* 51

∗

∾ **IV.2** *Drum. Enter Brutus, Lucius, and the Army.*
Lucillius, Titinius, and Pindarus meet them.

BRUTUS   Stand, ho!   1
SOLDIER   *(To a subordinate)* Give the word "ho," and stand. 2
BRUTUS
What now, Lucillius: is Cassius near?
LUCILLIUS
He is at hand, and Pindarus is come
To do you salutation from his master.
BRUTUS
He greets me well. Your master, Pindarus,   6
In his own change or by ill officers,   7
Hath given me some worthy cause to wish   8
Things done undone. But if he be at hand,
I shall be satisfied.   10
PINDARUS   I do not doubt
But that my noble master will appear
Such as he is, full of regard and honor.   12
BRUTUS
He is not doubted. A word, Lucillius.   13

---

48 *at the stake* i.e., like a bear at the stake bayed by dogs   51 *mischiefs*
schemes to harm us
    IV.2 Brutus's tent in his army's camp, near Sardis, in what is now western
Turkey   1 *Stand, ho* halt   2 *Give . . . "ho"* pass the word down the line to halt
6 *greets me well* sends his greetings by a worthy man   7 *In . . . officers*
whether from changed feelings on his part or through the acts of unworthy
subordinates   8 *worthy* justifiable   10 *be satisfied* receive a full explanation
12 *Such* exactly; *full . . . honor* regardful (of your interests) and honorable
13 *A word* i.e., tell me

Brutus and Lucillius speak apart.

14   How he received you let me be resolved.

LUCILLIUS

  With courtesy and with respect enough,

16   But not with such familiar instances,

17   Nor with such free and friendly conference,

  As he hath used of old.

BRUTUS   Thou hast described

19   A hot friend cooling. Ever note, Lucillius:

20   When love begins to sicken and decay

21   It useth an enforcèd ceremony.

22   There are no tricks in plain and simple faith;

23   But hollow men, like horses hot at hand,

24   Make gallant show and promise of their mettle;

    Low march within.

  But when they should endure the bloody spur,

26   They fall their crests and, like deceitful jades,

27   Sink in the trial. Comes his army on?

LUCILLIUS

28   They mean this night in Sardis to be quartered.

29   The greater part, the horse in general,

30   Are come with Cassius.

    Enter Cassius and his Powers.

BRUTUS   Hark, he is arrived.

31   March gently on to meet him.

    The Armies march.

CASSIUS

  Stand, ho!

---

14 *resolved* fully informed   16 *familiar instances* signs of friendship   17 *conference* conversation   19 *Ever note* always observe   21 *enforcèd ceremony* strained formality   22 *tricks* artifices   23 *hollow* insincere; *hot at hand* spirited at the start   24 *mettle* high spirit; **s.d.** *Low march within* soft drumbeat offstage (presumably it grows progressively louder over the next six lines)   26 *fall* let fall; *crests* ridges of horses' necks; *jades* nags   27 *Sink . . . trial* fail when they are put to the test   28 *Sardis* (the capital of the ancient kingdom of Lydia, in western Asia Minor; Brutus had requested Cassius to join forces with him there)   29 *horse in general* all the cavalry   30 **s.d.** *Powers* armies   31 *gently* slowly

BRUTUS
  Stand, ho! Speak the word along.
FIRST SOLDIER   Stand!
SECOND SOLDIER   Stand!
THIRD SOLDIER   Stand!
CASSIUS
  Most noble brother, you have done me wrong.
BRUTUS
  Judge me, you gods: wrong I mine enemies?
  And if not so, how should I wrong a brother?
CASSIUS
  Brutus, this sober form of yours hides wrongs,   40
  And when you do them –   41
BRUTUS   Cassius, be content.
  Speak your griefs softly. I do know you well.   42
  Before the eyes of both our armies here,
  Which should perceive nothing but love from us,
  Let us not wrangle. Bid them move away.
  Then in my tent, Cassius, enlarge your griefs,   46
  And I will give you audience.   47
CASSIUS   Pindarus,
  Bid our commanders lead their charges off   48
  A little from this ground.
BRUTUS
  Lucillius, do you the like; and let no man   50
  Come to our tent till we have done our conference.
  Let Lucius and Titinius guard our door.
                                   Exeunt the Armies.
      Brutus and Cassius remain, with Titinius and Lucius
      guarding the door.
CASSIUS
  That you have wronged me doth appear in this:
  You have condemned and noted Lucius Pella   54
  For taking bribes here of the Sardians,

---

40 *sober form* serious and restrained manner   **41** *content* calm   **42** *griefs* grievances   **46** *enlarge* express fully   **47** *audience* a hearing   **48** *charges* troops   **54** *noted* publicly disgraced, slandered

56   Wherein my letters praying on his side,
57   Because I knew the man, was slighted off.
BRUTUS
      You wronged yourself to write in such a case.
CASSIUS
59   In such a time as this it is not meet
60   That every nice offense should bear his comment.
BRUTUS
      Let me tell you, Cassius, you yourself
62   Are much condemned to have an itching palm,
63   To sell and mart your offices for gold
      To undeservers.
CASSIUS   I, an itching palm?
      You know that you are Brutus that speaks this,
66   Or, by the gods, this speech were else your last.
BRUTUS
67   The name of Cassius honors this corruption,
      And chastisement doth therefore hide his head.
CASSIUS
      Chastisement?
BRUTUS
70   Remember March, the ides of March, remember.
      Did not great Julius bleed for justice' sake?
      What villain touched his body, that did stab,
73 ⚡ And not for justice? What, shall one of us,
      That struck the foremost man of all this world
75   But for supporting robbers, shall we now
      Contaminate our fingers with base bribes,
77   And sell the mighty space of our large honors
78   For so much trash as may be graspèd thus?
79   I had rather be a dog and bay the moon

---

56 *letters* (singular in meaning)   57 *slighted off* contemptuously dismissed
59 *meet* appropriate   60 *nice . . . comment* trivial offense should be criticized
62 *condemned to have* accused of having; *itching palm* i.e., a covetous disposition   63 *mart* traffic in   66 *else* otherwise   67 *honors* lends an appearance
of honor to   73 *And not* except   75 *supporting robbers* (Caesar was accused
of permitting corruption among his subordinates)   77 *large honors* impres-
sive reputations   78 *trash* money (contemptuous)   79 *bay* howl at

Than such a Roman.   80

CASSIUS   Brutus, bay not me.
I'll not endure it. You forget yourself
To hedge me in. I am a soldier, I,   82
Older in practice, abler than yourself
To make conditions.   84

BRUTUS
Go to, you are not, Cassius.

CASSIUS
I am.

BRUTUS
I say you are not.

CASSIUS
Urge me no more, I shall forget myself.   88
Have mind upon your health. Tempt me no farther.   89

BRUTUS
Away, slight man.   90

CASSIUS
Is't possible?

BRUTUS
Hear me, for I will speak.
Must I give way and room to your rash choler?   93
Shall I be frighted when a madman stares?   94

CASSIUS
O ye gods, ye gods! Must I endure all this?

BRUTUS
All this? Ay, more. Fret till your proud heart break.
Go show your slaves how choleric you are,   97
And make your bondmen tremble. Must I budge?   98
Must I observe you? Must I stand and crouch   99
Under your testy humor? By the gods,   100

---

80 *bay not me* (1) do not howl at me, (2) do not (try to) hold me at bay   82
hedge me in i.e., limit my authority   84 *make conditions* manage affairs   88
Urge provoke   89 *health* safety; *Tempt* provoke   90 *slight* worthless   93
way . . . choler course and scope to your rash anger   94 *stares* glares   97 *choleric* angry   98 *budge* flinch   99 *observe* wait upon obsequiously; *crouch* cringe   100 *testy humor* irritable temper

101 You shall digest the venom of your spleen,
  Though it do split you. For from this day forth
103 I'll use you for my mirth, yea for my laughter,
  When you are waspish.

CASSIUS   Is it come to this?

BRUTUS
  You say you are a better soldier.
106 Let it appear so, make your vaunting true,
  And it shall please me well. For mine own part,
108 I shall be glad to learn of noble men.

CASSIUS
  You wrong me every way, you wrong me, Brutus.
110 I said an elder soldier, not a better.
  Did I say better?

BRUTUS   If you did, I care not.

CASSIUS
112 When Caesar lived he durst not thus have moved me.

BRUTUS
113 Peace, peace; you durst not so have tempted him.

CASSIUS
  I durst not?

BRUTUS
  No.

CASSIUS
  What, durst not tempt him?

BRUTUS
  For your life you durst not.

CASSIUS
  Do not presume too much upon my love.
  I may do that I shall be sorry for.

BRUTUS
120 You have done that you should be sorry for.
  There is no terror, Cassius, in your threats,

For I am armed so strong in honesty   122
That they pass by me as the idle wind,
Which I respect not. I did send to you   124
For certain sums of gold, which you denied me;
For I can raise no money by vile means.
By heaven, I had rather coin my heart
And drop my blood for drachmas than to wring
From the hard hands of peasants their vile trash
By any indirection. I did send   130
To you for gold to pay my legions,
Which you denied me. Was that done like Cassius?
Should I have answered Caius Cassius so?
When Marcus Brutus grows so covetous
To lock such rascal counters from his friends,   135
Be ready, gods, with all your thunderbolts;
Dash him to pieces.
CASSIUS   I denied you not.
BRUTUS
    You did.
CASSIUS   I did not. He was but a fool
    That brought my answer back. Brutus hath rived my   139
    heart.
    A friend should bear his friend's infirmities,   140
    But Brutus makes mine greater than they are.
BRUTUS
    I do not, till you practice them on me.
CASSIUS
    You love me not.
BRUTUS   I do not like your faults.
CASSIUS
    A friendly eye could never see such faults.
BRUTUS
    A flatterer's would not, though they do appear
    As huge as high Olympus.

---

122 *honesty* integrity   124 *respect not* ignore   130 *indirection* irregular, devious means   135 *rascal counters* base coins   139 *rived* broken

CASSIUS
    Come, Antony and young Octavius, come,
148 Revenge yourselves alone on Cassius;
    For Cassius is aweary of the world,
150 Hated by one he loves, braved by his brother,
151 Checked like a bondman; all his faults observed,
152 Set in a notebook, learned and conned by rote,
153 To cast into my teeth. O, I could weep
    My spirit from mine eyes! There is my dagger,
    And here my naked breast; within, a heart
156 Dearer than Pluto's mine, richer than gold.
    If that thou beest a Roman, take it forth.
    I that denied thee gold will give my heart.
    Strike as thou didst at Caesar; for I know
160 When thou didst hate him worst, thou loved'st him
      better
    Than ever thou loved'st Cassius.
    BRUTUS   Sheathe your dagger.
162 Be angry when you will; it shall have scope.
163 Do what you will; dishonor shall be humor.
164 O Cassius, you are yokèd with a lamb
    That carries anger as the flint bears fire,
166 Who, much enforcèd, shows a hasty spark
167 And straight is cold again.
    CASSIUS   Hath Cassius lived
    To be but mirth and laughter to his Brutus
169 When grief and blood ill-tempered vexeth him?
    BRUTUS
170 When I spoke that, I was ill-tempered too.
    CASSIUS
    Do you confess so much? Give me your hand.

---

148 *alone* solely   150 *braved* defied   151 *Checked* scolded   152 *conned by rote* memorized   153 *cast . . . teeth* i.e., throw up to me   156 *Dearer . . . mine* more precious than the riches within the earth (Pluto, god of the underworld, probably confused with Plutus, god of riches)   162 *it* i.e., your anger; *scope* free play   163 *dishonor . . . humor* I shall take your insults as an effect of your hot temper   164 *yokèd* allied   166 *enforcèd* worked on   167 *straight* at once   169 *blood ill-tempered* unbalanced disposition

BRUTUS
   And my heart too.
      They embrace.
CASSIUS   O Brutus!
BRUTUS   What's the matter?
CASSIUS
   Have not you love enough to bear with me
   When that rash humor which my mother gave me   174
   Makes me forgetful?
BRUTUS   Yes, Cassius, and from henceforth,
   When you are overearnest with your Brutus,
   He'll think your mother chides, and leave you so.   177
      Enter Lucillius and a Poet.
POET
   Let me go in to see the generals.
   There is some grudge between 'em; 'tis not meet   179
   They be alone.   *180*
LUCILLIUS   You shall not come to them.
POET
   Nothing but death shall stay me.
CASSIUS   How now! What's the
   matter?
POET
   For shame, you generals, what do you mean?
   Love and be friends, as two such men should be,
   For I have seen more years, I'm sure, than ye.
CASSIUS
   Ha, ha! How vilely doth this cynic rhyme!   185
BRUTUS   *To the Poet*
   Get you hence, sirrah; saucy fellow, hence!   186
CASSIUS
   Bear with him, Brutus, 'tis his fashion.

---

174 *humor* temper   177 *mother* i.e., inherited temperament (also hysteria?);
leave you so leave it at that   179 *grudge* ill feeling   185 *cynic* boorish fellow
186 *sirrah* (contemptuous form of address); *saucy* insolent

BRUTUS
188   I'll know his humor when he knows his time.
189   What should the wars do with these jigging fools?
        To the Poet
190   Companion, hence!
CASSIUS
        To the Poet
                                Away, away, be gone!
                                                Exit Poet.

BRUTUS
        Lucillius and Titinius, bid the commanders
        Prepare to lodge their companies tonight.
CASSIUS
        And come yourselves, and bring Messala with you
        Immediately to us.   *Exeunt Lucillius and Titinius.*
BRUTUS   Lucius, a bowl of wine.
                                                Exit Lucius.

CASSIUS
        I did not think you could have been so angry.
BRUTUS
196   O Cassius, I am sick of many griefs.
CASSIUS
        Of your philosophy you make no use,
198   If you give place to accidental evils.
BRUTUS
        No man bears sorrow better. Portia is dead.
CASSIUS
200   Ha! Portia?
BRUTUS
        She is dead.
CASSIUS
202   How scaped I killing when I crossed you so?

----

188 *I'll . . . time* I'll accept his fashion of behavior when he knows the proper
time and place for it   189 *jigging* rhyming (contemptuous), doggerel versi-
fying   190 *Companion* fellow (contemptuous)   196 *sick of* suffering from
198 *place* way; *accidental evils* evils caused by chance (i.e., Brutus, as a Stoic,
should not be affected by those external adversities caused by chance)   202
killing being killed (by you); *crossed* opposed

O insupportable and touching loss!   203
Upon what sickness?   204
BRUTUS   Impatience of my absence,
And grief that young Octavius with Mark Antony
Have made themselves so strong – for with her death   206
That tidings came. With this, she fell distraught,
And, her attendants absent, swallowed fire.   208
CASSIUS
And died so?   209
BRUTUS   Even so.
CASSIUS   O ye immortal gods!
Enter Lucius, with wine and tapers.
BRUTUS
Speak no more of her. *(To Lucius)* Give me a bowl of   210
wine.
      To Cassius
In this I bury all unkindness, Cassius.   211
      Brutus drinks.
CASSIUS
My heart is thirsty for that noble pledge.
Fill, Lucius, till the wine o'erswell the cup.   213
I cannot drink too much of Brutus' love.   214
      Cassius drinks.

                                              Exit Lucius.

      Enter Titinius and Messala.
BRUTUS
Come in, Titinius; welcome, good Messala.
Now sit we close about this taper here,
And call in question our necessities.   217

---

203 *touching* grievous   204 *Upon* as a result of; *Impatience of* unable to endure   206–8 *for . . . came* for together with the news of her death came that
news (of their strength)   208 *swallowed fire* (according to Plutarch, as trans-
lated by North, she cast "hot burning coals [from a charcoal brazier] . . . into
her mouth and kept her mouth so close that she choked herself")   209 s.d.
tapers candles   211 *In . . . unkindness* in this wine I'll drown all our differences   213 *o'erswell* overflow   214 s.d. *Messala* (Lucillius, whom, from ll.
191–94, we would expect to return at this point, is not mentioned; this inconsistency points to revision of this passage)   217 *call in question* discuss

CASSIUS *Aside, but heard by Brutus*
  Portia, art thou gone?
BRUTUS *Aside to Cassius*
                              No more, I pray you.
    They sit.
  Messala, I have here receivèd letters
220 That young Octavius and Mark Antony
221 Come down upon us with a mighty power,
222 Bending their expedition toward Philippi.
MESSALA
  Myself have letters of the selfsame tenor.
BRUTUS
  With what addition?
MESSALA
225 That by proscription and bills of outlawry
  Octavius, Antony, and Lepidus
  Have put to death an hundred senators.
BRUTUS
  Therein our letters do not well agree.
  Mine speak of seventy senators that died
230 By their proscriptions, Cicero being one.
CASSIUS
  Cicero one?
MESSALA   Ay, Cicero is dead,
  And by that order of proscription.
    To Brutus
233 Had you your letters from your wife, my lord?
BRUTUS
  No, Messala.
MESSALA
  Nor nothing in your letters writ of her?
BRUTUS
  Nothing, Messala.

---

221 *upon* against; *power* army 222 *Bending* hastily moving; *expedition* rapid march 225 *proscription* condemnation to death; *bills of outlawry* proscription lists 233–42 *Had . . . Portia* (the inconsistency of this passage with ll. 199–210 points to incomplete authorial revision)

MESSALA   That methinks is strange.
BRUTUS
  Why ask you? Hear you aught of her in yours?
MESSALA
  No, my lord.
BRUTUS
  Now as you are a Roman, tell me true.
MESSALA
  Then like a Roman bear the truth I tell;   *240*
  For certain she is dead, and by strange manner.
BRUTUS
  Why, farewell, Portia. We must die, Messala.
  With meditating that she must die once,   *243*
  I have the patience to endure it now.
MESSALA
  Even so great men great losses should endure.
CASSIUS
  I have as much of this in art as you,   *246*
  But yet my nature could not bear it so.   *247*
BRUTUS
  Well, to our work alive. What do you think   *248*
  Of marching to Philippi presently?   *249*
CASSIUS
  I do not think it good.   *250*
BRUTUS   Your reason?
CASSIUS   This it is:
  'Tis better that the enemy seek us;
  So shall he waste his means, weary his soldiers,
  Doing himself offense; whilst we, lying still,   *253*
  Are full of rest, defense, and nimbleness.
BRUTUS
  Good reasons must of force give place to better.   *255*
  The people 'twixt Philippi and this ground

---

243 *once* at some time   246 *I . . . you* i.e., from my philosophical studies
(*art*) I have learned as much of Stoical fortitude as you   247 *nature* natural
emotions   248 *alive* that concerns us as living men   249 *presently* immediately   253 *offense* injury   255 *of force* of necessity

257 Do stand but in a forced affection,
258 For they have grudged us contribution.
     The enemy marching along by them
260 By them shall make a fuller number up,
261 Come on refreshed, new added, and encouraged;
     From which advantage shall we cut him off,
     If at Philippi we do face him there,
     These people at our back.
CASSIUS   Hear me, good brother.
BRUTUS
265 Under your pardon. You must note beside
     That we have tried the utmost of our friends;
     Our legions are brimful, our cause is ripe.
     The enemy increaseth every day;
     We at the height are ready to decline.
270 ☛There is a tide in the affairs of men
     Which, taken at the flood, leads on to fortune;◆
272 Omitted, all the voyage of their life
273 Is bound in shallows and in miseries.
     On such a full sea are we now afloat,
     And we must take the current when it serves,
276 Or lose our ventures.
CASSIUS   Then, with your will, go on.
     We'll along ourselves, and meet them at Philippi.
BRUTUS
     The deep of night is crept upon our talk,
     And nature must obey necessity,
280 Which we will niggard with a little rest.
     There is no more to say.
CASSIUS   No more. Good night.
282 Early tomorrow will we rise and hence.

---

257 *Do . . . affection* favor us only by compulsion   258 *contribution* money
(to support the army)   261 *new added* reinforced   265 *Under your pardon*
allow me to continue   272 *Omitted* not taken   273 *bound in* confined to
276 *ventures* investments risked on the high seas; *with your will* as you wish
280 *niggard* stint (i.e., sleep only a short time)   282 *hence* go from here

BRUTUS
   Lucius.   283
      Enter Lucius.
         My gown.   *Exit Lucius.*
            Farewell, good Messala.
   Good night, Titinius. Noble, noble Cassius,
   Good night and good repose.
CASSIUS   O my dear brother,
   This was an ill beginning of the night!
   Never come such division 'tween our souls.
   Let it not, Brutus.
      Enter Lucius with the gown.
BRUTUS   Everything is well.
CASSIUS
   Good night, my lord.
BRUTUS   Good night, good brother.
TITINIUS, MESSALA
   Good night, Lord Brutus.   290
BRUTUS   Farewell, every one.
         Exeunt Cassius, Titinius, and Messala.
   Give me the gown.   291
      He puts on the gown.
            Where is thy instrument?
LUCIUS
   Here in the tent.
BRUTUS   What, thou speak'st drowsily.
   Poor knave, I blame thee not; thou art o'erwatched.   293
   Call Claudio and some other of my men.
   I'll have them sleep on cushions in my tent.
LUCIUS
   Varrus and Claudio!
      Enter Varrus and Claudio.
VARRUS   Calls my lord?

---

283 *gown* dressing gown   **291** *instrument* i.e., probably a lute or cithern
293 *knave* lad (affectionate); *o'erwatched* stayed up too long (and tired from lack of sleep)

BRUTUS

I pray you, sirs, lie in my tent and sleep.

298 It may be I shall raise you by and by

On business to my brother Cassius.

VARRUS

300 So please you, we will stand and watch your pleasure.

BRUTUS

I will not have it so. Lie down, good sirs.

302 It may be I shall otherwise bethink me.

Varrus and Claudio lie down to sleep.

Look, Lucius, here's the book I sought for so.

I put it in the pocket of my gown.

LUCIUS

I was sure your lordship did not give it me.

BRUTUS

Bear with me, good boy, I am much forgetful.

Canst thou hold up thy heavy eyes a while,

308 And touch thy instrument a strain or two?

LUCIUS

309 Ay, my lord, an't please you.

BRUTUS   It does, my boy.

310 I trouble thee too much, but thou art willing.

LUCIUS

It is my duty, sir.

BRUTUS

I should not urge thy duty past thy might.

313 I know young bloods look for a time of rest.

LUCIUS

I have slept, my lord, already.

BRUTUS

It was well done, and thou shalt sleep again.

316 I will not hold thee long. If I do live,

I will be good to thee.

---

298 *raise* awaken; *by and by* soon   300 *stand* stay awake; *watch your pleasure*
attend to you   302 *otherwise bethink me* change my mind   308 *touch* play
on; *strain* musical composition   309 *an't* if it   313 *young bloods* youthful
constitutions   316 *hold* detain

Lucius plays a tune and sings a song. He slowly falls
asleep, and as he does so, the music stops.
This is a sleepy tune.   318
    Noticing the sleeping boy
                        O murd'rous slumber,
Lay'st thou thy leaden mace upon my boy   319
That plays thee music?   320
    To the sleeping Lucius
                        Gentle knave, good night.
I will not do thee so much wrong to wake thee.
If thou dost nod thou break'st thy instrument;
I'll take it from thee, and, good boy, good night.
    He takes away Lucius' instrument, then opens the
    book.
Let me see, let me see, is not the leaf turned down
Where I left reading? Here it is, I think.
    Enter the Ghost of Caesar.
How ill this taper burns! Ha! Who comes here?   326
I think it is the weakness of mine eyes   327
That shapes this monstrous apparition.
It comes upon me. Art thou any thing?   329
Art thou some god, some angel, or some devil,   330
That mak'st my blood cold and my hair to stare?   331
Speak to me what thou art.
CAESAR'S GHOST
    Thy evil spirit, Brutus.
BRUTUS
    Why com'st thou?
CAESAR'S GHOST
    To tell thee thou shalt see me at Philippi.
BRUTUS
    Well; then I shall see thee again?

---

318 *murd'rous* giving the appearance of death   319 *leaden mace* heavy staff
of office   326 *How . . . burns* (it was commonly held that lights burned dim
or blue in the presence of a ghost or spirit; in an open theater it was impossible to lower the lights, so the dimming had to be suggested verbally)   327
weakness . . . eyes i.e., possibly a hallucination   329 *upon* toward   331 *stare*
stand on end

CAESAR'S GHOST   Ay, at Philippi.
BRUTUS
Why, I will see thee at Philippi then.
                                   Exit Caesar's Ghost.
Now I have taken heart, thou vanishest.
Ill spirit, I would hold more talk with thee.
    Calling
340   Boy, Lucius, Varrus, Claudio, sirs, awake!
Claudio!
LUCIUS   *Awakening*
              The strings, my lord, are false.
BRUTUS
He thinks he still is at his instrument.
Lucius, awake!
LUCIUS
My lord.
BRUTUS
Didst thou dream, Lucius, that thou so cried'st out?
LUCIUS
My lord, I do not know that I did cry.
BRUTUS
Yes, that thou didst. Didst thou see anything?
LUCIUS   Nothing, my lord.
BRUTUS
Sleep again, Lucius. Sirrah Claudio! *(To Varrus)* Fellow,
350   Thou, awake!
VARRUS   *(Awakening)* My lord.
CLAUDIO   *(Awakening)* My lord.
BRUTUS
Why did you so cry out, sirs, in your sleep?
VARRUS, CLAUDIO
Did we, my lord?
BRUTUS   Ay. Saw you anything?
VARRUS
No, my lord, I saw nothing.
CLAUDIO   Nor I, my lord.

———
340 *false* out of tune

BRUTUS
   Go and commend me to my brother Cassius.   356
   Bid him set on his powers betimes before,   357
   And we will follow.
VARRUS, CLAUDIO   It shall be done, my lord.

> *Exeunt Varrus and Claudio*
> *at one door, Brutus and*
> *Lucius at another door.*

*

∾ **V.1** *Enter Octavius, Antony, and their Army.*

OCTAVIUS
   Now, Antony, our hopes are answerèd.
   You said the enemy would not come down,
   But keep the hills and upper regions.
   It proves not so; their battles are at hand.   4
   They mean to warn us at Philippi here,   5
   Answering before we do demand of them.   6
ANTONY
   Tut, I am in their bosoms, and I know   7
   Wherefore they do it. They could be content   8
   To visit other places; and come down
   With fearful bravery, thinking by this face   10
   To fasten in our thoughts that they have courage;   11
   But 'tis not so.
     Enter a Messenger.
MESSENGER   Prepare you, generals.
   The enemy comes on in gallant show.   13

---

356 *commend me* give my greetings   **357** *set on* advance; *betimes before* early
in the morning, before me
   V.1 The remainder of the play takes place on the battlefield near Philippi,
a city in northeastern Greece.   **4** *proves* turns out to be; *battles* armies   **5**
warn challenge   **6** *Answering . . . them* appearing against us before we call
them to combat   **7** *in their bosoms* know their secrets (i.e., he has spies in
their army)   **8–9** *could . . . places* would prefer to be elsewhere   **10** *fearful
bravery* display that inspires fear in the enemy and conceals one's own fear;
face defiance   **11** *fasten* fix the idea   **13** *gallant* splendid

14   Their bloody sign of battle is hung out,
15   And something to be done immediately.

ANTONY

16   Octavius, lead your battle softly on
      Upon the left hand of the even field.

OCTAVIUS

      Upon the right hand, I; keep thou the left.

ANTONY

19   Why do you cross me in this exigent?

OCTAVIUS

20   I do not cross you, but I will do so.
            Drum. Antony and Octavius march with their Army.
            Drum within. Enter, marching, Brutus, Cassius, and
            their Army, amongst them Titinius, Lucillius, and
            Messala. Octavius and Antony's Army makes a stand.

BRUTUS

      They stand, and would have parley.

CASSIUS

22   Stand fast, Titinius. We must out and talk.
            Brutus and Cassius' Army makes a stand.

OCTAVIUS

      Mark Antony, shall we give sign of battle?

ANTONY

24   No, Caesar, we will answer on their charge.
25   Make forth, the generals would have some words.

OCTAVIUS   *To his Army*

      Stir not until the signal.
            Antony and Octavius meet Brutus and Cassius.

BRUTUS

      Words before blows: is it so, countrymen?

OCTAVIUS

      Not that we love words better, as you do.

---

14 *bloody sign* red flag   15 *to* is to   16 *battle* army; *softly* slowly, warily   19
cross oppose; *exigent* critical moment   20 *cross* march on the right side of; *I
will do so* I will dispute with you (in the future)   22 *out* go forward   24 *on
their charge* when they attack   25 *Make forth* go forward

BRUTUS
    Good words are better than bad strokes, Octavius.
ANTONY
    In your bad strokes, Brutus, you give good words.   30
    Witness the hole you made in Caesar's heart,
    Crying "Long live, hail Caesar."
CASSIUS   Antony,
    The posture of your blows are yet unknown;   33
    But for your words, they rob the Hybla bees,   34
    And leave them honeyless.
ANTONY
    Not stingless too.
BRUTUS
    O yes, and soundless too,
    For you have stolen their buzzing, Antony,
    And very wisely threat before you sting.
ANTONY
    Villains, you did not so when your vile daggers   40
    Hacked one another in the sides of Caesar.
    You showed your teeth like apes, and fawned like hounds,   42
    And bowed like bondmen, kissing Caesar's feet,
    Whilst damnèd Casca, like a cur, behind,
    Struck Caesar on the neck. O you flatterers!
CASSIUS
    Flatterers? Now, Brutus, thank yourself.
    This tongue had not offended so today
    If Cassius might have ruled.   48
OCTAVIUS
    Come, come, the cause. If arguing make us sweat,   49
    The proof of it will turn to redder drops.   50
        He draws.
    Look, I draw a sword against conspirators.
    When think you that the sword goes up again?   52

---

30 *In your* i.e., as you deliver   33 *posture* fashion, quality   34 *Hybla* (a Sicil-
ian town famous for the sweetness of its honey)   40 *so* i.e., give warning   42
showed your teeth grinned obsequiously   48 *ruled* had his way (at II.1.155–
61)   49 *the cause* to our business   50 *proof* trial   52 *goes up* will be sheathed

Never till Caesar's three and thirty wounds
54   Be well avenged, or till another Caesar
55   Have added slaughter to the swords of traitors.

BRUTUS
Caesar, thou canst not die by traitors' hands,
57   Unless thou bring'st them with thee.

OCTAVIUS   So I hope.
I was not born to die on Brutus' sword.

BRUTUS
59   O, if thou wert the noblest of thy strain,
60   Young man, thou couldst not die more honorable.

CASSIUS
61   A peevish schoolboy, worthless of such honor,
62   Joined with a masquer and a reveler!

ANTONY
Old Cassius still.

OCTAVIUS   Come, Antony, away.
Defiance, traitors, hurl we in your teeth.
If you dare fight today, come to the field.
66   If not, when you have stomachs.

Exeunt Octavius, Antony,
and their Army.

CASSIUS
67   Why, now blow wind, swell billow, and swim bark.
68   The storm is up, and all is on the hazard.

BRUTUS
Ho, Lucillius! Hark, a word with you.

LUCILLIUS   My lord.
He comes forward, and speaks privately with Brutus.

CASSIUS
70   Messala.

---

54 *another Caesar* i.e., himself   **55** *Have . . : to* has also been killed by   **57** *Unless . . . thee* i.e., unless by your hand   **59** *strain* line of descent   **61** *peevish* childish (Octavius was twenty-one); *worthless* unworthy   **62** *masquer . . . reveler* i.e., Antony, who was well known for his love of extravagant entertainments and banquets (see II.1.189, II.2.116)   **66** *stomachs* appetite (for battle)   **67** *bark* ship   **68** *on the hazard* at stake

MESSALA   *Standing forth*
           What says my general?
CASSIUS   Messala,
   This is my birthday; as this very day   71
   Was Cassius born. Give me thy hand, Messala.
   Be thou my witness that, against my will,
   As Pompey was, am I compelled to set   74
   Upon one battle all our liberties.
   You know that I held Epicurus strong,   76
   And his opinion. Now I change my mind,
   And partly credit things that do presage.   78
   Coming from Sardis, on our former ensigns   79
   Two mighty eagles fell, and there they perched,   80
   Gorging and feeding from our soldiers' hands,
   Who to Philippi here consorted us.   82
   This morning are they fled away and gone,
   And in their steads do ravens, crows, and kites   84
   Fly o'er our heads and downward look on us,
   As we were sickly prey. Their shadows seem   86
   A canopy most fatal, under which   87
   Our army lies ready to give the ghost.   88
MESSALA
   Believe not so.   89
CASSIUS   I but believe it partly,
   For I am fresh of spirit, and resolved   90
   To meet all perils very constantly.   91
BRUTUS
   Even so, Lucillius.
CASSIUS   *Joining Brutus*
                    Now, most noble Brutus,

---

71 *as* on   74 *As Pompey was* (at Pharsalus, where he was persuaded to fight
Caesar against his will); *set* stake, gamble   76–77 *held . . . opinion* was a con-
vinced follower of the Epicurean philosophy (i.e., a materialist, who thought
it foolishly superstitious to believe in omens)   78 *credit* believe in   79 *former* foremost; *ensigns* standards, banners   80 *fell* swooped down, alighted
82 *consorted* accompanied   84 *ravens . . . kites* scavengers that proverbially
anticipate death   86 *As* as if; *sickly* dying   87 *fatal* ominous, foreboding
death   88 *give* give up   89 *but* only   91 *constantly* resolutely

93   The gods today stand friendly, that we may,
94   Lovers in peace, lead on our days to age.
95   But since the affairs of men rest still incertain,
96   Let's reason with the worst that may befall.
     If we do lose this battle, then is this
     The very last time we shall speak together.
99   What are you then determinèd to do?

BRUTUS

100   Even by the rule of that philosophy
     By which I did blame Cato for the death
     Which he did give himself – I know not how,
     But I do find it cowardly and vile
104   For fear of what might fall so to prevent
105   The time of life – arming myself with patience
106   To stay the providence of some high powers
     That govern us below.

CASSIUS   Then if we lose this battle,

108   You are contented to be led in triumph
109   Thorough the streets of Rome?

BRUTUS

110   No, Cassius, no.
     Think not, thou noble Roman,
112   That ever Brutus will go bound to Rome.
     He bears too great a mind. But this same day
     Must end that work the ides of March begun;
     And whether we shall meet again I know not.
     Therefore our everlasting farewell take.
     For ever and for ever farewell, Cassius.
     If we do meet again, why, we shall smile.

---

93 *The . . . friendly* may the gods be well disposed toward us today   **94** *Lovers* dear friends   **95** *rest still* remain always   **96** *reason . . . befall* consider what to do if the worst should happen   **99** *then* i.e., if we should lose   **100** *that philosophy* i.e., Plato, who rejected suicide   **104** *fall* happen; *prevent* anticipate   **105** *time* natural limit   **106** *stay* wait for; *providence* destiny; *some* whatever (i.e., Brutus does not believe in the Roman gods, but he does believe in *powers,* whose nature he cannot exactly define)   **108** *in triumph* in a victory procession (as a captive)   **109** *Thorough* through   **112** *bound* in chains (as a captive)

If not, why then, this parting was well made.

CASSIUS

For ever and for ever farewell, Brutus.   *120*
If we do meet again, we'll smile indeed.
If not, 'tis true this parting was well made.

BRUTUS

Why then, lead on. O that a man might know
The end of this day's business ere it come!
But it sufficeth that the day will end,
And then the end is known.

> *To his troops*   Come, ho, away!   *Exeunt.*

*

❧ **V.2** *Alarum. Enter Brutus and Messala.*

BRUTUS

Ride, ride, Messala, ride, and give these bills   1
Unto the legions on the other side.   2
> *Loud alarum.*

Let them set on at once, for I perceive   3
But cold demeanor in Octavio's wing,   4
And sudden push gives them the overthrow.   5
Ride, ride, Messala; let them all come down.   6

> *Exeunt severally.*

*

❧ **V.3** *Alarums. Enter Cassius with an ensign, and
Titinius.*

CASSIUS

O look, Titinius, look: the villains fly.   1
Myself have to mine own turned enemy: 2

V.2 The battlefield **s.d.** *Alarum* a drum signal calling to arms   **1** *bills* written orders   **2** *the other side* Cassius's wing (of the army)   **3** *set on* advance   **4** *cold demeanor* lack of spirit (in battle)   **5** *push* assault; *gives . . . overthrow* will defeat them   **6** *them . . . down* the whole army attack
  V.3 The battlefield **s.d.** *ensign* banner   **1** *villains* i.e., my own troops   **2** *mine own* my own men

3   This ensign here of mine was turning back;
4   I slew the coward, and did take it from him.
TITINIUS
    O Cassius, Brutus gave the word too early,
6   Who, having some advantage on Octavius,
7   Took it too eagerly. His soldiers fell to spoil,
    Whilst we by Antony are all enclosed.
      Enter Pindarus.
PINDARUS
    Fly further off, my lord, fly further off!
10   Mark Antony is in your tents, my lord;
11   Fly therefore, noble Cassius, fly farre off.
CASSIUS
    This hill is far enough. Look, look, Titinius,
    Are those my tents where I perceive the fire?
TITINIUS
    They are, my lord.
CASSIUS   Titinius, if thou lovest me,
    Mount thou my horse, and hide thy spurs in him
    Till he have brought thee up to yonder troops
    And here again, that I may rest assured
    Whether yon troops are friend or enemy.
TITINIUS
19   I will be here again even with a thought.   *Exit.*
CASSIUS
20   Go, Pindarus, get higher on that hill.
21   My sight was ever thick. Regard Titinius,
22   And tell me what thou not'st about the field.
                    Exit Pindarus.
    This day I breathèd first. Time is come round,
    And where I did begin, there shall I end.
25   My life is run his compass.
      Enter Pindarus on the upper stage.

---

3 *ensign* standard-bearer 4 *it* i.e., the standard he was bearing 6 *on* over
7 *spoil* looting 10 *tents* encampment 11 *farre* farther (the obsolete comparative of "far") 19 *even . . . thought* in the twinkling of an eye 21 *thick* poor; *Regard* observe 22 *not'st* note, observe 25 *is . . . compass* has completed its full circuit

                          Sirrah, what news?
PINDARUS
  O my lord!
CASSIUS
  What news?
PINDARUS
  Titinius is enclosèd round about
  With horsemen, that make to him on the spur.   29
  Yet he spurs on. Now they are almost on him.   30
  Now Titinius. Now some light. O, he lights too.   31
  He's ta'en.   32
      Shout within.
  And hark, they shout for joy.
CASSIUS   Come down; behold no
      more.
                                        Exit Pindarus.
  O coward that I am, to live so long
  To see my best friend ta'en before my face!
      Enter Pindarus below, on the main stage.
  Come hither, sirrah. In Parthia did I take thee prisoner,
  And then I swore thee, saving of thy life,   37
  That whatsoever I did bid thee do
  Thou shouldst attempt it. Come now, keep thine oath.
  Now be a freeman, and, with this good sword   40
  That ran through Caesar's bowels, search this bosom.   41
  Stand not to answer. Here, take thou the hilts,   42
      Pindarus takes the sword.
  And when my face is covered, as 'tis now,
  Guide thou the sword.
      Pindarus stabs him.
                          Caesar, thou art revenged,
  Even with the sword that killed thee.
      He dies.

---

29 *make to* approach; *on the spur* rapidly   31 *light . . . lights* dismount . . .
dismounts   32 *ta'en* captured   37 *swore thee* made you swear; *saving of* when
I spared   41 *search* prove, penetrate into   42 *Stand* delay; *hilts* sword handle

PINDARUS

46   So, I am free, yet would not so have been
47   Durst I have done my will. O Cassius!
      Far from this country Pindarus shall run,
      Where never Roman shall take note of him.   *Exit.*
      Enter Titinius, wearing a laurel-leaf wreath of victory,
      and Messala.

MESSALA

50   It is but change, Titinius, for Octavius
      Is overthrown by noble Brutus' power,
      As Cassius' legions are by Antony.

TITINIUS

53   These tidings will well comfort Cassius.

MESSALA

      Where did you leave him?

TITINIUS   All disconsolate,
      With Pindarus his bondman, on this hill.

MESSALA

      Is not that he that lies upon the ground?

TITINIUS

      He lies not like the living. O, my heart!

MESSALA

      Is not that he?

TITINIUS   No, this was he, Messala;
      But Cassius is no more. O setting sun,

60   As in thy red rays thou dost sink tonight,
      So in his red blood Cassius' day is set.
      The sun of Rome is set. Our day is gone.
      Clouds, dews, and dangers come. Our deeds are done.

64   Mistrust of my success hath done this deed.

MESSALA

      Mistrust of good success hath done this deed.

66   O hateful Error, Melancholy's child,

---

46 *not so* not in such circumstances   47 *Durst* dared; *my will* (rather than
Cassius's will, which he was sworn to do)   50 *change* an exchange, "quid pro
quo"   53 *comfort* encourage   64 *Mistrust . . . success* doubt about the out-
come of my mission   66 *Melancholy's child* (melancholy persons fear unreal
dangers)

Why dost thou show to the apt thoughts of men   67
The things that are not? O Error, soon conceived,
Thou never com'st unto a happy birth,
But kill'st the mother that engendered thee.   70

TITINIUS
What, Pindarus! Where art thou, Pindarus?

MESSALA
Seek him, Titinius, whilst I go to meet
The noble Brutus, thrusting this report
Into his ears. I may say "thrusting" it,
For piercing steel and darts envenomèd   75
Shall be as welcome to the ears of Brutus
As tidings of this sight.   77

TITINIUS   Hie you, Messala,
And I will seek for Pindarus the while.   *Exit Messala.*
Why didst thou send me forth, brave Cassius?   79
Did I not meet thy friends, and did not they   80
Put on my brows this wreath of victory,
And bid me give it thee? Didst thou not hear their shouts?
Alas, thou hast misconstrued everything.
But hold thee, take this garland on thy brow.   84
Thy Brutus bid me give it thee, and I
Will do his bidding. Brutus, come apace,   86
And see how I regarded Caius Cassius.   87
By your leave, gods, this is a Roman's part: 88
Come Cassius' sword, and find Titinius' heart.
   He stabs himself, and dies.
   Alarum. Enter Brutus, Messala, young Cato, Strato,
   Volumnius, Lucillius, Labeo, and Flavius.

BRUTUS
Where, where, Messala, doth his body lie?   90

MESSALA
Lo yonder, and Titinius mourning it.

---

67 *apt* impressionable   70 *mother* i.e., the melancholy person who conceived the error   75 *darts* spears   77 *Hie* hurry   79 *brave* noble   84 *hold
thee* wait a minute   86 *apace* quickly   87 *regarded* respected, honored, es-
teemed   88 *leave* permission; *part* role, function (in such circumstances)

BRUTUS
   Titinius' face is upward.
CATO   He is slain.
BRUTUS
   O Julius Caesar, thou art mighty yet.
   Thy spirit walks abroad, and turns our swords
95 In our own proper entrails.
          Low alarums.
CATO   Brave Titinius,
96 Look whe'er he have not crowned dead Cassius.
BRUTUS
   Are yet two Romans living such as these?
   The last of all the Romans, fare thee well.
   It is impossible that ever Rome
100 Should breed thy fellow. Friends, I owe more tears
   To this dead man than you shall see me pay.
          To Cassius' body
   I shall find time, Cassius, I shall find time.
          To his men
103 Come, therefore, and to Thasos send his body.
   His funerals shall not be in our camp,
105 Lest it discomfort us. Lucillius, come;
   And come, young Cato. Let us to the field.
107 Labeo and Flavius, set our battles on.
   'Tis three o'clock, and, Romans, yet ere night
   We shall try fortune in a second fight.
                              Exeunt with the bodies.

                    *

---

95 *own proper* very own; **s.d.** *Low* soft; *Brave* noble   96 *whe'er* whether   103
Thasos (an island near Philippi, where, according to Plutarch, Cassius was
buried)   105 *discomfort us* dishearten our army   107 *battles* forces

❧ **V.4** *Alarum. Enter Brutus, Messala, young Cato,*
Lucillius, and Flavius.

BRUTUS
　Yet, countrymen, O yet hold up your heads.
　　　　　　　　　Exit with Messala and Flavius.
CATO
　What bastard doth not? Who will go with me?　　　2
　I will proclaim my name about the field.
　I am the son of Marcus Cato, ho!
　A foe to tyrants, and my country's friend.　　　5
　I am the son of Marcus Cato, ho!
　　Enter Soldiers, and fight.
LUCILLIUS
　And I am Brutus, Marcus Brutus, I,
　Brutus, my country's friend. Know me for Brutus.
　　Soldiers kill Cato.
　O young and noble Cato, art thou down?
　Why, now thou diest as bravely as Titinius,　　　10
　And mayst be honored, being Cato's son.
FIRST SOLDIER
　Yield, or thou diest.　　　　　　　　　　12
LUCILLIUS　　　　　　Only I yield to die.
　There is so much, that thou wilt kill me straight:　　13
　Kill Brutus, and be honored in his death.
FIRST SOLDIER
　We must not. A noble prisoner.
SECOND SOLDIER
　Room, ho! Tell Antony Brutus is ta'en.
　　Enter Antony.
FIRST SOLDIER
　I'll tell the news. Here comes the general.
　　To Antony

V.4 The battlefield　**2** *What bastard* who is so lowborn that he　**5** *tyrants*
(such as Caesar and his followers)　**10** *bravely* nobly　**12** *Only . . . die* I sur-
render only in order to die　**13** *so much* so great an inducement to honor and
fame; *straight* at once

Brutus is ta'en, Brutus is ta'en, my lord.

ANTONY
Where is he?

LUCILLIUS
20   Safe, Antony, Brutus is safe enough.
I dare assure thee that no enemy
Shall ever take alive the noble Brutus.
The gods defend him from so great a shame.
24   When you do find him, or alive or dead,
25   He will be found like Brutus, like himself.

ANTONY   *To First Soldier*
This is not Brutus, friend, but, I assure you,
A prize no less in worth. Keep this man safe.
Give him all kindness. I had rather have
Such men my friends than enemies.
         To another Soldier   Go on,
30   And see whe'er Brutus be alive or dead,
And bring us word unto Octavius' tent
32   How everything is chanced.

> *Exeunt the Soldier at one door,*
> *Antony, Lucillius and other Soldiers,*
> *some bearing Cato's body, at another door.*

                    *

∾ **V.5**   *Enter Brutus, Dardanius, Clitus, Strato, and*
Volumnius.

BRUTUS
1   Come, poor remains of friends, rest on this rock.
      He sits. Strato rests and falls asleep.

CLITUS
2   Statillius showed the torchlight, but, my lord,
3   He came not back. He is or ta'en or slain.

---

24 *or* either   25 *like himself* true to his noble nature   32 *is chanced* has happened
V.5 The battlefield   1 *poor remains* pitiful survivors   2 *Statillius . . . torchlight* i.e., a scout who got as far as Cassius's encampment, occupied by Antony's troops, from which he signaled   3 *or ta'en* either captured

BRUTUS
Sit thee down, Clitus. Slaying is the word:
It is a deed in fashion. Hark thee, Clitus.
  He whispers.
CLITUS
What I, my lord? No, not for all the world.
BRUTUS
Peace, then, no words.
CLITUS   I'll rather kill myself.
  He stands apart.
BRUTUS
Hark thee, Dardanius.
  He whispers.
DARDANIUS   Shall I do such a deed?
  He joins Clitus.
CLITUS
O Dardanius!
DARDANIUS
O Clitus!   *10*
CLITUS
What ill request did Brutus make to thee?
DARDANIUS
To kill him, Clitus. Look, he meditates.
CLITUS
Now is that noble vessel full of grief,   *13*
That it runs over even at his eyes.
BRUTUS
Come hither, good Volumnius. List a word.   *15*
VOLUMNIUS
What says my lord?
BRUTUS   Why this, Volumnius.
The ghost of Caesar hath appeared to me
Two several times by night – at Sardis once,   *18*
And this last night, here in Philippi fields.
I know my hour is come.   *20*

---

13 *noble vessel* completely noble man (also a sacred vessel for holding the tears of devout mourners) 15 *List* hear 18 *several* different

VOLUMNIUS   Not so, my lord.

BRUTUS
Nay, I am sure it is, Volumnius.
Thou seest the world, Volumnius, how it goes.
23   Our enemies have beat us to the pit,
      Low alarums.
24   It is more worthy to leap in ourselves
      Than tarry till they push us. Good Volumnius,
      Thou know'st that we two went to school together.
      Even for that, our love of old, I prithee,
      Hold thou my sword hilts whilst I run on it.

VOLUMNIUS
That's not an office for a friend, my lord.
      Alarum still.

CLITUS
30   Fly, fly, my lord! There is no tarrying here.

BRUTUS
Farewell to you, and you, and you, Volumnius.
Strato, thou hast been all this while asleep.
      Strato wakes.
Farewell to thee too, Strato. Countrymen,
My heart doth joy that yet in all my life
I found no man but he was true to me.
I shall have glory by this losing day,
More than Octavius and Mark Antony
38   By this vile conquest shall attain unto.
39   So fare you well at once, for Brutus' tongue
40   Hath almost ended his life's history.
      Night hangs upon mine eyes. My bones would rest,
42   That have but labored to attain this hour.
      Alarum. Cry within: "Fly, fly, fly!"

CLITUS
Fly, my lord, fly!

---

23 *beat* driven; *the pit* a trap into which a wild animal is driven in order to be captured (with a pun on "the grave")   **24** *more worthy* nobler   **38** *vile conquest* i.e., the destruction of Republican Rome   **39** *at once* all together   **42** *but labored* worked toward no other end than

BRUTUS   Hence; I will follow.
                              Exeunt Clitus, Dardanius,
                                       and Volumnius.
   I prithee, Strato, stay thou by thy lord.
   Thou art a fellow of a good respect.   45
   Thy life hath had some smatch of honor in it.   46
   Hold then my sword, and turn away thy face
   While I do run upon it. Wilt thou, Strato?
STRATO
   Give me your hand first. Fare you well, my lord.
BRUTUS
   Farewell, good Strato.   50
      Strato holds the sword, while Brutus runs on it.
                        Caesar, now be still.
   I killed not thee with half so good a will.   51
      He dies.
      Alarum. Retreat.
      Enter Antony, Octavius, Messala, Lucillius, and the
      Army.
OCTAVIUS
   What man is that?
MESSALA
   My master's man. Strato, where is thy master?   53
STRATO
   Free from the bondage you are in, Messala.
   The conquerors can but make a fire of him,   55
   For Brutus only overcame himself,   56
   And no man else hath honor by his death.
LUCILLIUS
   So Brutus should be found. I thank thee, Brutus,
   That thou hast proved Lucillius' saying true.
OCTAVIUS
   All that served Brutus, I will entertain them.   60

---

45 *respect* reputation   **46** *smatch* relish   **51 s.d.** *Retreat* trumpet signal to
cease pursuit   **53** *man* servant   **55** *make a fire of* cremate   **56** *Brutus only
overcame* only Brutus defeated   **60** *entertain them* take them into my service

To Strato

61   Fellow, wilt thou bestow thy time with me?

STRATO

62   Ay, if Messala will prefer me to you.

OCTAVIUS

    Do so, good Messala.

MESSALA   How died my master, Strato?

STRATO

    I held the sword, and he did run on it.

MESSALA

65   Octavius, then take him to follow thee,

66   That did the latest service to my master.

ANTONY

    This was the noblest Roman of them all.

    All the conspirators save only he

69   Did that they did in envy of great Caesar.

70   He only in a general honest thought

71   And common good to all made one of them.

72   His life was gentle, and the elements

73   So mixed in him that nature might stand up

74   And say to all the world "This was a man."

OCTAVIUS

75   According to his virtue let us use him,

    With all respect and rites of burial.

    Within my tent his bones tonight shall lie,

78   Most like a soldier, ordered honorably.

79   So call the field to rest, and let's away

80   To part the glories of this happy day.

                         Exeunt with Brutus' body.

---

61 *bestow* spend   62 *prefer* recommend   65 *follow* serve   66 *latest* last, final
69 *that* what   70–71 *in . . . all* with an honorable purpose and for the good
of all Romans   71 *made . . . them* joined the conspiracy   72 *gentle* noble;
elements the four elements (earth, water, air, and fire, of which all matter was
thought to be composed, or the four corresponding humors: melancholic,
phlegmatic, sanguine, and choleric; in the ideal individual, no single humor
predominated)   73 *So mixed* i.e., equally balanced   74 *a man* i.e., an ideal
man   75 *According* in accordance with; *use* treat   78 *ordered* treated   79
field army   80 *part* share, divide